Public and Professional Attitudes Toward AIDS Patients

Public and Professional Attitudes Toward AIDS Patients

A National Dilemma

Cornell University Medical College
(Fifth) Conference on Health Policy, 5th

EDITED BY

David E. Rogers and Eli Ginzberg

WITHDRAW[

WESTVIEW PRESS
BOULDER • SAN FRANCISCO • LONDON

Copyright © 1989 by Cornell University Medical College

Published in 1989 in the United States of America by Westview Press, Inc., 5500 Central Avenue, Boulder, Colorado 80301, and in the United Kingdom by Westview Press, Inc., 13 Brunswick Centre, London WC1N 1AF, England

Library of Congress Cataloging-in-Publication Data
Cornell University Medical College Conference on Health Policy (5th : 1989 : New York, N.Y.)
  Public and professional attitudes toward AIDS patients : a national dilemma / Cornell University Medical College Fifth Conference on Health Policy; edited by David E. Rogers and Eli Ginzberg.
    p.   cm.
  Includes bibliographical references.
  ISBN 0-8133-7861-3
  1. AIDS (Disease)—Patients—United States—Public opinion—Congresses.   2. AIDS (Disease)—Government policy—United States—Congresses.   3. AIDS (Disease)—Patients—Care—United States—Congresses.   I. Rogers, David E. (David Elliott), 1926–   .
II. Ginzberg, Eli, 1911–   .   III. Title.
RA644.A25C67   1989
362.1'9697'9200973—dc20   89-22462
                                                                                              CIP

Printed and bound in the United States of America

⊗   The paper used in this publication meets the requirements of the American National Standard for Permanence of Paper for Printed Library Materials Z39.48-1984.

10   9   8   7   6   5   4   3   2

Contents

Introduction

David E. Rogers

This volume analyzes in considerable depth how fears, prejudices, social and moral values, and individual perceptions have affected and shaped the public, the personal, the professional, and the economic ways in which our society interacts with people suffering from human immunodeficiency virus (HIV) infections. A central consideration is how well our society has responded to this dreadful epidemic that initially emerged primarily among two groups—gay men and intravenous (IV) drug users—whose life-styles are distasteful or condemned by many in our society.

Chapters explore how well our society has handled frightening epidemic plagues in the past; what characterizes public attitudes toward people with acquired immune deficiency syndrome (AIDS) today, after nine years of experience with the disease; how health professionals feel about patients with HIV infections; and how they are coping personally both with patients and with their own concerns about transmission of the virus. Other chapters consider how hospitals, ethicists, lawyers, and public officials are reacting to the medical crisis of our times.

It has been painfully apparent to all of us who have worked in this area that our first nine years of experience with AIDS have some powerful lessons to teach us. As has been true with all epidemics during recorded human history, our response to AIDS has been a result of the play of many forces—rumors, science-based knowledge, social values, religious beliefs, local mores, and the political tenor of the times. But with AIDS there have been some notable differences. Thanks to the remarkable advances we have made in basic biomedical science during the past several decades, we know vastly more about the infectious agent, how to detect its presence, and what it does to the human organism than was true of any previous plague. But, paradoxically—and in part because of the rapid acquisition of knowledge about the particular groups of people among whom AIDS first emerged—social attitudes and judgmental values have tended to overwhelm science-based knowledge in determining our response to the epidemic.

In modern society we have come to expect medical science to speedily develop technical solutions to problems of illness. Usually, we absorb such technological fixes swiftly and easily. So it was a keen disappointment when, early on, there was clear evidence that there would be no easy or rapid biomedical answer—no antiviral agent or vaccine—to solve the problem of AIDS. However, there was evidence that education leading to behavioral change and appropriate responses at a social and political level could help control the spread of the disease. Still, for the reasons already outlined, educational and behavioral responses have been difficult to set in motion and implement. Though we adapt rapidly to new technologies, change is slow when it involves altering our attitudes, our values, and our social and behavioral patterns.

This volume focuses on exploring in considerable detail changes in attitudes and behavior that must occur if we are to respond adequately to the AIDS epidemic. We must learn to deal more effectively with the fears, prejudices, and mind-sets that have too often blocked our progress in coping with AIDS.

This publication expresses many insights about how our society can soften the harshness with which it has dealt with people with AIDS and how we can be more effective in controlling the disease. Despite the enormous individual efforts expended so far to care for those ill and dying with HIV infection, the public response to the HIV epidemic has been tragically slow, too little, and too lacking in urgency. This book aims to show how the American people can cope better and more generously with the scourge of AIDS as well as to strengthen support for those responsible for our public health. Over the long haul, our society may well be judged by how well it responds to this all-too-human crisis. It deserves our best efforts.

1

An Overview

Eli Ginzberg

The principal goals of this introductory chapter are to provide the reader with some background for the selection of the theme for the Fifth Cornell University Medical College Conference on Health Policy; to highlight the major thrusts of the ten conference papers; and to call attention to gains in understanding that took place as the result of lively discussions among the authors of the papers and the participants over the two-day conference.

The fourth Cornell conference, held in February, 1988, addressed "The AIDS Patient: An Action Agenda." Sixteen speakers from federal, state, and local government, and from the nongovernmental sector, attempted to focus the attention of the public and decision-makers on the growing problems that AIDS patients and the community confront as the epidemic continues to spread.

In planning the conference for 1989, David Rogers and I recognized that one important dimension of an effective response to the AIDS crisis was the need to consider the relationship between the AIDS patient and the health professional. The centrality of the relationship was underscored by the following: reports of growing shortages of professional personnel, particularly nurses and support personnel; reports of difficulties that New York teaching hospitals faced in attracting residents because a growing proportion of their medical-surgical beds were filled with AIDS patients; surveys and other reports indicating the reluctance of some health personnel to treat and care for AIDS patients because of fears of infection or strong distaste for the life-styles that had led these patients to contract the disease; and complex problems in the therapeutic environment including the difficulties of maintaining the confidentiality of patients' records, the need for strict infection-control methods, the complexities entailed in constructing and financing long-term care facilities in urban areas in the face of neighborhood opposition, and an array of additional problems in establishing and expanding adequate systems of care for different groups of AIDS patients. This list of problem areas in the relationship between the AIDS patient and health professionals provides the rationale for the fifth Cornell conference.

The first five chapters illuminate directly and specifically the attitudes of health professionals toward AIDS patients, discuss legal and ethical concerns, and provide a historical view of public responses to infectious disease. Kenneth Ludmerer helped set the framework for the discussion by noting that societal response to earlier epidemics had often been to blame the victims for having contracted the disease—a precondition for limiting society's responsibility to provide succor. Moreover, physicians' behavior often left much to be desired; some fled the locales where epidemics raged to avoid contracting the disease, while others remained to treat the sick, often for monetary reasons.

Robert Blendon discussed the realities that emerged from an extensive analysis of opinion research surveys: Americans with AIDS face discrimination because of the hostile attitude of large segments of the population; the result is the loss of jobs, housing, and ready access to health care for the afflicted.

M. Roy Schwarz, drawing primarily on attitude surveys conducted by the American Medical Association, called attention to the substantial minority of physicians who reported strong feelings of homophobia; the significant group who expressed fear of contracting AIDS as a result of treating AIDS patients; the substantial proportion who favored mandatory reporting and contact tracing; and the sizable minority, one out of four, who hold the belief that physicians are not ethically bound to treat AIDS patients.

Gayling Gee, a registered nurse with long experience at San Francisco General Hospital, reviewed the literature dealing with nurses' attitudes toward AIDS. She called attention to the following trends: the growing concern of nurses about contracting the disease, even in the face of substantial educational efforts showing the low probability of transmission to caregivers; the extent to which many nurses, like many physicians, are uncomfortable in dealing with homosexual patients; and the pressures on nurses from family and friends to discontinue contacts with AIDS patients. About one in four nurses reported that he or she would "absolutely not accept a job caring for AIDS patients," and an additional 10 percent would do so only "very reluctantly."

Troyen Brennan addressed the critical question of whether reliance on the law or ethics would better remove barriers to health care for patients with HIV-related disease. He has decided unequivocally in favor of the law, contending that in the absence of a common morality in our society, it is difficult, if not impossible, to rely on ethical principles and professional ethics to assure appropriate professional behavior. He discussed the effectiveness of legal sanctions, but he also emphasized the advantages of using incentives, particularly the availability of liberal disability and life insurance, to assure health-care workers that in the event of their becoming infected, they would not also suffer grievous economic harm.

The remaining five chapters move beyond the specific issues involved in the attitudes and behavior of health professionals and look at such broader issues as the ability of New York City hospitals to respond effectively to the growing crisis of AIDS patients, the need for strengthened national and state policy on AIDS, and the economics of a caring approach. The last chapter provides advice from one of the nation's leading medical researchers.

Thomas Killip, drawing heavily on his experience as the executive vice president and medical director of the Beth Israel Medical Center in New York City, provided an array of facts that emphasized the extent to which the hospitals in that city are strained because of a governmentally directed reduction of 1,800 beds in the early 1980s, combined with subsequent unexpectedly large admissions for patients suffering from psychiatric disorders, drug abuse, and AIDS. It is urgent that the present gridlock be relieved if disaster is to be avoided: The number of AIDS cases is projected to increase from 17,600 in 1988 to 76,700 by 1994. Improved micro-hospital management, additional nursing home beds, adequate home care, greater cooperation among the city's medical centers, and improved coordination between the public and the private sector are imperative if the hospital system is to survive.

Bruce C. Vladeck focused his chapter, "The Economics of a Caring Approach," on such important themes as the connections between poverty and ill health, including the economic risks facing AIDS patients and their need for income as well as health-services support; the limitations of exclusive reliance on Medicaid as the principal conduit of governmental assistance to AIDS patients; the desirability of federal block grant support; and the urgent necessity for the nation to recognize that while AIDS is currently concentrated disproportionately in a few cities and states, it should be responded to as a public health threat of concern to the entire population.

Theodore Cooper, who has chaired the ongoing committee on AIDS of the National Academy of Sciences, made available his group's recent letter to President George Bush that detailed the steps required to forge an effective national policy on AIDS. The more important recommendations include using the National Commission on Acquired Immune Deficiency Syndrome more effectively; protecting HIV-infected persons against discrimination; strengthening the financing of care of AIDS patients; fortifying efforts to treat individuals suffering from substance abuse; expanding educational efforts; controlling testing, surveillance, and research; and, finally, engaging in international cooperation to control the disease.

A long-time, deeply involved legislator, Richard Gottfried, noted that New York State policy has both its strong and weak points. On the positive side, it set up the AIDS Institute in 1983 and passed legislation in 1988 to tighten confidentiality. On the down side, the state faces a severe budgetary crunch, which has ominous consequences for health care in general and AIDS in particular. In searching for a compromise between the need for more funding for health care and Governor Mario Cuomo's determination to keep a lid on new taxes, Gottfried saw a glimmer of hope in the introduction of some longer-term plans in Albany that will address the immediate problems, even if most of the new funding would come later on.

Lewis Thomas emphasized two points: the immensity of the threat that faces not only the United States but the whole world, once full account is taken of the magnitude of the epidemic raging in Africa; and the consequent urgent necessity for the American people and their elected representatives to mount appropriate responses to this steadily growing scourge that has not yet peaked and is unlikely to do so soon. Moreover, he thought it highly unlikely that medical research would be able to interdict the continued growth of AIDS. He was equally pessimistic about the likelihood that education would lead to behavioral changes sufficiently effective to contain the spread of the virus.

Additional points of both illumination and uncertainty arose from the active interchanges among the authors of the chapters and the other conference participants. The first relates to the difficulty of maintaining the focus of discussion on the AIDS patient and on the steps required to assist those either exposed to or stricken with the disease. The discussion tended to veer off to such related matters as shortages of hospital and home-care services available in New York City, particularly for low-income individuals, and the extent to which race and class dominate the world of AIDS and influence the directions of private and public policy. Some argued that it might prove necessary to reform the health-care system via national health insurance. Others expressed the need for the elimination of racism as a precondition to, or concomitant to, adequate care for AIDS patients and a halt to the spread of the epidemic. Once these spill-over relationships were recognized and appraised, the conferees concluded that the campaign for effective treatment of AIDS patients should not be submerged in such contentious issues as national health insurance or an intensified struggle to eliminate racism.

A second troublesome area that forced its way onto the agenda related to the reasons for the low level of interest, concern, and support of most of the American public for a national AIDS policy such as that advocated in the letter from the National Academy of Sciences to President Bush. As this subject was explored, it became increasingly clear that the American people have not been convinced that a serious problem of nationwide scale and scope exists or that the existing evidence justifies intensified intervention. The public remembers the episode in the mid-1970s of the swine flu epidemic, which raised a scare that never materialized. In the face of this current widespread skepticism about the present and future extent of the AIDS epidemic, a critical need exists for the medical profession to reach an early consensus about the gravity of the present situation and its probable near- and longer-term effects and, subsequent to pressure on the federal government, to take the leadership in broadening its epidemiological studies so that the American people can have the benefit of reliable knowledge of present and future threats from AIDS. This is a clear priority.

To reinforce the above: Currently most Americans believe that AIDS is a disease centered in two patient groups—gay males and IV drug addicts—and that five cities—San Francisco, Los Angeles, Miami, Newark, and, above all, New York—are home to most of the patients in need of treatment. From this the public makes a further assumption: The people between the east and west coasts have little if anything to fear, since AIDS is restricted to these specific populations and therefore represents little or no threat to the white heterosexual population. But these assumptions and projections, based on limited information, are likely to be proven wrong. The consequence may be that the entire population suddenly finds itself at risk.

Belatedly, but nonetheless surely, Congress has moved from miserly to relatively liberal appropriations for two of the three areas of pressing need—educational programs to reduce the spread of the disease and biomedical research—in the hope and expectation of speeding the discovery of agents of sufficient potency to limit the spread of the virus and to reverse the natural course of the disease. But Congress has done relatively little to assist the states and the localities where the disease is currently concentrated and where it is placing increasing burdens on local health-care institutions and on state and local governments.

Congress cannot continue to ignore the fact that a growing emergency is confronting the four states with the largest numbers of AIDS patients. These states face a growing health and financial emergency that warrants federal intervention and assistance. The concept of emergency aid for the victims of catastrophe is a foundation of U.S. democracy and needs to be applied to the present AIDS crisis.

2

Patients Beyond the Pale: A Historical View

Kenneth M. Ludmerer

The appearance of the acquired immune deficiency syndrome (AIDS) in the 1980s represents one of the greatest ironies in the history of medicine. The germ theory of disease, enunciated over 100 years ago, at long last allowed sense to be made of infectious illness and rationalized the public health movement. In the decades that followed, a spate of new vaccines and antisera were developed. In the 1930s and 1940s the discovery of sulfonamide and penicillin inaugurated the present antibiotic age and allowed the cure as well as the prevention of most bacterial diseases.[1] With the appearance in the 1970s of Legionnaires' disease and the toxic shock syndrome, medical scientists again demonstrated the power of their methods by identifying with amazing rapidity the new infectious agents, methods of diagnosis, and drugs for treatment.

AIDS ruptured this sense of medical security. Not since the influenza pandemic of 1918–1919, which claimed no fewer than twenty-one million lives worldwide, had epidemic disease reached such frightening proportions.[2] AIDS was terrifying to the very core: a contagious disease without cure that was inevitably fatal. In this context it is not difficult to understand why the social response to AIDS has been so much deeper and more lasting than the response to the highly publicized epidemics of venereal disease, such as herpes, chlamydia, and penicillin-resistant cases of gonorrhea, in the early 1980s. Only in AIDS are the vital elements of dread and fear present.

But the biological behavior of AIDS explains only in part the inordinate social response it has evoked. The total number of deaths in the United States attributable to AIDS is only one-tenth of the number of deaths each year caused by cancer—a disease that itself has evoked no small amount of fear and has become enshrouded with mystique and social metaphor.[3] However, as many have commented, AIDS is perceived as a demeaning disease, as an affliction of socially marginal groups. According to Dorothy Nelkin and Stephen Hilgartner, "unclean body fluids, taboo sexual conduct, forbidden drugs, deviant individuals, and deadly disease become mutually reinforcing metaphors of physical, moral, and social danger."[4] The mass hysteria that surrounds AIDS has resulted in large measure from the fact that the disease has become a symbol of physical and moral degeneracy. Our society does not look charitably upon homosexuality and intravenous drug abuse, and those who have contracted AIDS have become social outcasts. They are patients beyond the pale.

These observations raise an important historical question: How well has Western society responded in the past to diseases that have affected individuals with life-styles distasteful to or condemned by the majority? It is common knowledge that the answer is "not very well"; the temptation to scapegoat is exceedingly strong, especially when society is confronted with a fatal, incurable disease of epidemic proportions. Historians and psychologists know that scapegoating has been one of the irrepressible constants in human behavior over time.

In this chapter I shall focus upon an even more intriguing question, one with special relevance to the AIDS debate: How does society decide which individuals to scapegoat? In most major epidemics there have been patients beyond the pale; what has differed from one epidemic to another is the matter of who has been deemed beyond the pale—and why. Because the forms scapegoating takes are culturally determined, they tell us much about the values, prejudices, and biases of a given society. Recognition of this cultural determinant of illness is crucial if the metaphors surrounding AIDS are to be stripped away and U.S. society is to respond to AIDS in the most compassionate, just, and scientifically potent fashion.

Socially Stigmatized Groups

People in the twentieth century have become accustomed to good health. With current human life expectancy in the mid-seventies, and with the diseases of aging representing the most common causes of death, citizens of industrialized nations have been spared the brutish realities of the human condition that characterized life from the beginning of history through the early twentieth century. Until only recently, pain, suffering, disease, and premature death were harsh realities of human life. Societies were ravaged by epidemic and endemic illness; towns and villages were decimated by plague, small pox, cholera, malaria, and yellow fever; parents saw their children taken from them by influenza, diphtheria, and scarlet fever; and young adults regularly died from pneumonia and tuberculosis. In 1800 in the United States, the life expectancy at birth was only thirty years; by 1900 that figure was still less than fifty years. Only in the 1920s, when the public health measures we so readily take for granted today became universally implemented, did life expectancy greatly increase.[5]

During almost all epidemics before the twentieth century, doctors stood helpless to prevent the disease from spreading or to provide effective treatment to the afflicted. Medical theory offered erudite explanations for disease: The bubonic plague represented an excess production of black bile; cholera resulted from an imbalance between individuals and their environment. Yet speculative theory did not translate into effective prevention or treatment, and epidemic diseases proceeded virtually unchecked. Smallpox, after the discovery of variolation in the eighteenth century, was the sole exception.[6]

When medicine stands ineffective in the face of dread disease, the temptation to explain disease in cultural terms is pervasive and overwhelming. Society gains comfort and hope in feeling that outsiders or socially disapproved groups are in some way responsible for the outbreak of disease. If those groups can be placed beyond the pale of society—via stigmatization, isolation, quarantine, or genocide—the epidemic might be brought under control.

Throughout history, however, such draconian measures have generally failed to stem the progress of epidemic disease. Instead, they have served only as a vent for society's deep-seated fears and prejudices toward the outcast groups. I shall illustrate this temptation to blame socially marginal groups with examples from different societies at different times in history. In each case, disease served as a focus for the expression of the religious, political, and cultural biases of a given society.

In ancient Greece, the cardinal sin was to be hopelessly ill from any malady. Greeks revered the healthy and strong; they had little compassion for the lame, infirm, or terminally ill. The highest social good was health; the greatest curse was illness. The physician held an exalted social position, for the role of medicine was to restore the ailing individual to health. However, if the condition was incurable, the sufferer could expect no mercy. The most practical solution was to destroy the weakling, and this was frequently done, either by infanticide or euthanasia. Medical care was reserved for those with the potential for recovery, and Greek physicians considered it unethical to provide care in a hopeless case.[7] Thus, as Henry Sigerist has observed, the sick man in Greek society "found himself burdened with an odium, not that of sin but of inferiority."[8]

Christian society adopted a much more humane view of illness. Jesus Christ had performed cures; according to Christian thought his disciples should attempt to do the same, and those who fell ill should be regarded as carrying a cross in the footsteps of the Lord. The protection and nurturing of the sick became embedded in the idea of Christian charity, and the Christian community assumed the duty of tending to the ill. It was this impulse that gave rise to the world's first hospitals. The sick person was no longer scorned, but was offered a preferential position in society. Sigerist has called this history's "most revolutionary and decisive change in the attitude of society toward the sick."[9]

However, Christian charity was put sorely to the test when epidemic disease struck. The most notorious pandemic of all time occurred in the fourteenth century when the bubonic plague, or Black Death, struck Europe. Outbreaks of plague had been occurring for nearly a millennium (and further outbreaks were to occur in the future), but at no time did the plague strike with greater force and brutality than in 1347. In the next four years the disease decimated Europe. By most estimates, one-third to one-half of the continent's population died. The disease was recognized to be contagious. Accordingly, entire populations of towns and villages fled at the first whisper of disease. Parents abandoned afflicted children, and husbands and wives deserted each other.[10]

Amid such pestilence and destruction, society broke down. Some people resorted to asceticism and prayer vigils; others threw themselves into licentiousness and riotous orgies. But, above all, society was angry and sought scapegoats. The Jews, who were hard-hit by the disease, were singled out. To some, Jews were heathens whose sacrilege had brought on the wrath of God. To others, Jews were selfish mercenaries whose worldly concern for business had provoked God's wrath. Still others, heavily indebted to Jewish bankers and merchants, saw mass genocide as a way to eliminate their hated creditors.[11] For all of these reasons, bands of flagellants roamed the streets throughout Europe and killed the Jews. The persecution was especially intense in southern Germany, where the homes of thousands of Jews were burned, killing the Jews within.

The New World, too, suffered killer epidemics. Small pox, yellow fever, cholera, and malaria affected the economy and culture of the United States as much as traditional political events. One of the most notorious outbreaks of disease in the United States was the cholera epidemic of 1832, the first of three devastating cholera epidemics to hit the country in the mid-nineteenth century. When cases of cholera were reported in New York City in the spring of 1832, people were terrified. As many as 100,000 of New York's 250,000 people fled the city any way they could—on foot, in boats, in stagecoaches, and even in wheelbarrows.

Medical thought at that time held cholera to be God's retribution for intemperate living and vice; the disease was considered by many to be just punishment for Sabbath-breaking, drunkenness, and debauchery. People were not surprised when the disease broke out in the slums of Manhattan's humid, marshy Lower East Side, where impoverished immigrants lived near the docks in crowded, decrepit, unfinished shacks and cellars, and where pigs and horses roamed freely in the streets. One contemporary observed that cholera victims constituted "the poorest class of Irish, many of [whom] have for years (as they themselves confessed) been almost daily intoxicated."[12] The disease was perceived as fitting retribution for the despised Irish immigrants who were leading such immoral, dissolute lives. Indeed, many felt that the victims did not need to be cared for. They hoped that cholera would claim the susceptible and that the disease would then die out on its own. In stark fashion, the harsh living conditions that made the Irish special prey to the disease vindicated the popular stereotypes and social prejudices that had made them a socially marginal group.

In contrast, when the disease spread in New York to the "respectable" middle class, doctors were perplexed. It was thought that middle-class victims, too, were being punished for having weakened their bodies through dissolute living. However, they were also widely viewed as innocent victims of the immoral Irish whose habits had allowed the disease to take seed and spread. The parallel with AIDS in contemporary American culture is obvious. Heterosexuals, hemophiliacs, and newborn infants who contract the disease are widely held to be the innocent victims of the homosexuals and intravenous drug users whose degenerate living in some way created the curse.[13]

As the Irish were blamed for the outbreak of cholera in New York City in 1832, the Italians were likewise blamed for the epidemic of poliomyelitis that erupted in the city in 1916. In that epidemic, a total of 8,927 cases were reported, with 2,343 deaths. (Nationwide, there were about 27,000 cases in 26 states, with 6,000 deaths.) The epidemic broke out in a poor, densely populated waterfront area of Brooklyn called "Pigtown," in the jargon of the day. Inhabited primarily by Italian immigrants, the Pigtown section of Brooklyn bore the brunt of the epidemic, and harsh measures of quarantine were imposed on many of the area's residents. Since the epidemic claimed the lives of a disproportionate number of Italian immigrants, this group was condemned for having introduced polio from their homeland—even though there was never any epidemiological evidence to substantiate that charge. Once again, prejudice proved stronger than reason; the ensuing vilification of Italians was the result of social prejudice rather than of medical understanding.[14]

The sad history of prejudice shows that epidemic disease is not a prerequisite for hatred and bigotry to masquerade as medical science. Nowhere is this more clearly illustrated than with the eugenics movement. In the United States in the early twentieth century, fear and hostility toward immigrants from southern, middle, and eastern Europe gave rise to the view that these groups were racially inferior and a biological threat to the germ plasm of the American people. In the United States, such thinking culminated with the enactment by many states of eugenic sterilization laws and with the passage by the federal government of the Immigration Restriction Act of 1924.[15] In Nazi Germany, the same thinking was carried much further and provided the biological ratio-nalization for euthanasia and mass genocide. The saddest and most shameful moment in the history of medicine was when German physicians gave their active support and leadership to eugenics in Nazi Germany.[16]

Socially Stigmatized Behavior

When medicine is powerless to control fatal disease, the prejudices of a society are laid bare, and groups are socially stigmatized. Such was the case with the infirm and terminally ill in Greek society, the Jews during the bubonic plague of 1347, the Irish during the cholera epidemic of 1832, and the Italians during the polio epidemic of 1916. However, just as socially stigmatized groups are vulnerable to being scapegoated, those who engage in socially stigmatized behavior are strongly condemned. No better example can be offered than the history of changing attitudes toward those who have contracted syphilis.

The origin of syphilis in Europe is obscure; all that is known for certain is that it appeared in epidemic form for the first time in 1493. For approximately three decades the venereal nature of the disease was not known; around 1520 it was recognized that the disease was sexually transmitted. For the next two-and-one-half centuries it was not considered shameful to have contracted syphilis. Renaissance attitudes toward sex were very liberal, and extramarital relations were both common and socially sanctioned, especially among the nobility. Love for one's wife was considered ridiculous; it was much more proper to inquire about another's mistress than about his spouse.

Accordingly, syphilis was rampant, particularly among the upper classes. Emperors, kings, noblemen, churchmen, scholars, and poets spoke openly of their illness; no one thought of concealing the fact that he had contracted the disease. The humanist Ulrich von Hutten wrote eloquently of his illness, describing his symptoms in great detail without shame or embarrassment. Erasmus of Rotterdam wrote that a nobleman who had not suffered from syphilis should be considered "ignoble and a rustic." Especially in the eighteenth century, a time of great sexual licentiousness, it became almost a badge of distinction to have contracted the disease. Syphilis became known as the cavalier's disease, and songs and verses were written about it. The symbols of the era were Don Juan and Casanova.[17]

With the rise of the middle class in the second half of the eighteenth century, new attitudes toward syphilis began to form. The bourgeoisie emphasized the sanctity of the family and the importance of premarital chastity and virtue. They condemned licentiousness, speaking of wantons and whores, not paramours and lady-loves. By adopting such a self-righteous attitude, the middle class could claim to be more virtuous than the aristocracy and, thus, clamor more strongly for greater social, economic, and political privilege.

By the nineteenth century, this new attitude toward syphilis had become dominant in Western society. Syphilis was now equated with sin, and one who acquired the disease disgraced himself and his family. The disease was shameful, not to be discussed aloud, especially in proper society. To the religious, syphilis was viewed as appropriate punishment for the victim's crime against morality.[18] This transformed view of syphilis clearly illustrates how strongly the definition of socially unacceptable behavior depends on the general culture of a society. Behavior that is stigmatized in one era or society is not necessarily taboo in another.

Yet, even with this new puritanical view of syphilis, not all sufferers from the disease were looked upon in the same way. Society continually differentiated between the guilty spreaders of infection and those who were their innocent victims. During World War I, for example, as syphilis became a major health problem in army camps, prostitutes who served the soldiers were villainized as unpatriotic defilers of the heroic American soldier. In what Allan Brandt called "the most concerted attack on civil liberties in the name of public health in America,"[19] prostitutes were routinely rounded up and tested for syphilis; those found to be infected were jailed or subjected to quarantine or detention. In contrast, soldiers would merely receive public health lectures and moral exhortations; those afflicted would be quietly treated and returned to duty.[20] Similarly, in public health discussions in Baltimore in the 1930s and 1940s, syphilis was commonly portrayed as a disease of immoral, lascivious blacks incapable of controlling their rapacious sexual desires—despite repeated observations by a few public health officials that "nice people" also contracted syphilis and that the disease should be regarded as a public health problem, not as a matter of sin and immorality.[21]

This history of cultural attitudes toward syphilis bears directly upon the controversy surrounding AIDS today. Socially stigmatized behavior is culturally defined. Just as Victorian attitudes toward sexuality differed sharply from those of the Renaissance, not every society has been as homophobic as ours. The acceptance of homosexuality in Greek society demonstrates this point. Similarly, the temptation to identify certain sufferers of a disease as moral infidels and others as innocent victims has been a frequent occurrence in history. Just as it condemned syphilis victims in the ninetheenth and twentieth centuries, U.S. society today condemns homosexuals and drug users who suffer from AIDS. Like the soldiers of World War I, others who have contracted AIDS receive some modicum of sympathy. Our attitudes toward AIDS, like our attitudes toward other epidemic diseases, reveal as much about ourselves as about the disease.

It is worth noting that the tendency to define vice selectively has also characterized the history of drug abuse in the United States. Stringent laws prohibiting the use of narcotics were passed in this country during the years around World War I; previously, the use of opium, cocaine, morphine, and heroin had been widespread and unrestricted. In the campaigns to criminalize drug use, the prejudices of U.S. society were again laid bare. According to David Musto, "Smoking opium was linked to Chinese immigrants, cocaine to southern blacks, heroin to an urban, violent, and criminal underclass. In the 1930s a similar specific assignment was made of marijuana to Mexican immigrants."[22] This attitude may be contrasted with the relative lack of emotion surrounding the widespread abuse of certain barbiturates and tranquilizers by the "respectable" middle class.[23]

Physician Behavior: Negotiation and Opportunity

Physicians are, above all, human. Confronted with deadly epidemics, they fear for their lives—and for those of their families—as do other mortals. As members of society, they are likely to share the dominant attitudes, values, and ethics of their culture. Thus, it would be naive to expect physicians, purely on the basis of their scientific training, to be any more tolerant of homosexuals and drug users than other educated persons, just as it would be equally naive to expect physicians of late Victorian-era America to have been any less prudish or less prejudiced toward immigrants than their contemporaries were.

These observations raise the question of how the medical profession carried out its duties in previous generations when confronted with diseases that terrorized every member of society. Some reports indicate that physicians' behavior in past epidemics was less than heroic. Galen fled Rome in the second century A.D. and Thomas Sydenham fled London when plague struck in the seventeenth century. In the United States, prominent physicians fled Philadelphia and New York when yellow fever appeared in the eighteenth century and cholera appeared in the nineteenth century. Many doctors who did not flee refused to attend those who were ill. Other reports, however, emphasized the self-sacrifices of the many doctors who did remain during past epidemics to tend to the sick and dying. No consistent pattern of professional behavior has emerged.[24]

Recently, Daniel M. Fox brought sense to the history of physician responsibility. Studying several of history's deadliest epidemics, he noted two constants: first, that a process of negotiation occurred between civic leaders and the medical community regarding who would treat the victims; and, second, that the epidemics provided doctors with opportunities as well as risks. Communities recruited physicians to provide care in times of epidemics by offering increased pay and, for doctors who survived, enhanced social and professional prestige. Doctors who responded to the call knew they were placing themselves in physical jeopardy, but they balanced this risk with the incentive of making more money and receiving public adulation. Physicians met society's need for medical care less out of ethical consciousness than in response to economic and social incentives. Not all doctors could be so lured, but in each epidemic that Fox studied, enough were lured that most of society's social objectives could be met.[25]

Today, as AIDS has caused health-care professionals to rediscover personal risk, it is likely that a similar contract between society and physicians will be made. It is improbable that many doctors will rush to treat AIDS patients for altruistic or ethical reasons. More likely, society will attract physicians to render the needed care by offering the same incentives as in the past: money and prestige. Rewards need not be strictly economic; academic medical scientists may be induced to care for AIDS patients by the prospect of receiving research grants and scholarly recognition. A pattern of behavior based on a negotiated contract between physicians and society, rather than one based on ethical precepts, is once again the most probable outcome.

Policy Implications: Exposing the Metaphors

The appearance of AIDS has illustrated that in modern times, as in the past, the meaning of disease is culturally as well as medically determined. To many Americans, homosexuality, not a retrovirus, is the cause of AIDS, and the disease is condign punishment for gay promiscuity. Since many "innocent victims" have contracted the disease, homosexuals are considered all the more reprehensible; they have placed the entire community at risk. The solution, according to this perverse logic, is to condemn and repress homosexual behavior.

If there is a lesson to be learned from history, it is the importance of exposing the metaphors so that the disease itself can be more objectively examined and effectively controlled. Public health is properly concerned with making bodies healthier, not minds more pure. The public must be taught that AIDS is not a disease of sexual preference but of sexual behavior and intravenous drug use and that heterosexuals can transmit the virus as well. Behavioral changes are needed, but these must be focused on helping individuals avoid contact with a pathogen, not on trying to enforce celibacy or repress homosexuality. Separating irrational fears from our scientific understanding is no easy task, so deeply rooted are these fears in our culture and attitudes. Nevertheless, lifting the metaphors is the only approach possible if the victims are to be treated compassionately and the epidemic brought under control.

Notes

The author wishes to acknowledge his appreciation to the Henry J. Kaiser Family Foundation for a research grant that helped support this work.

1. Harry F. Dowling, *Fighting Infection: Conquests of the Twentieth Century* (Cambridge, Mass.: Harvard University Press, 1977).

2. For an excellent account of the influenza pandemic of 1918-19, see Alfred W. Crosby, Jr., *Epidemic and Peace, 1918* (Westport, Conn.: Greenwood Press, 1976).

3. Susan Sontag, *Illness as Metaphor* (New York: Farrar, Straus and Giroux, 1978).

4. Dorothy Nelkin and Stephen Hilgartner, "Disputed Dimension of Risk," *The Milbank Quarterly* 64, supp. 1 (1986): 139.

5. A definitive history of public health remains to be written. A useful overview is George Rosen, *A History of Public Health* (New York: MD Publications, 1958).

6. The most sweeping history of smallpox is Donald R. Hopkins, *Princes and Peasants: Smallpox in History* (Chicago: University of Chicago Press, 1983).

7. On the duty of ancient doctors not to treat, see Erich H. Loewy, "Duties, Fears and Physicians," *Social Science and Medicine* 22 (1986): 1363–66; Darrel W. Amundsen, "Medical Deontology and Pestilential Disease in the Late Middle Ages," *Journal of the History of Medicine and Allied Sciences* 32 (1977): 403–21; Darrel W. Amundsen, "The Physician's Obligation to Prolong Life: A Medical Duty Without Classical Roots," *Hastings Center Report* 8, no. 4 (1978): 23–31; and J. Valsh, "Refutation of the Charges of Cowardice Against Galen," *Annals of Medical History* 3 (1931): 195–208.

8. Henry E. Sigerist, *Civilization and Disease* (Ithaca, N.Y.: Cornell University Press, 1943), p. 69 (quotation), pp. 68–69 (discussion of Greek medicine).

9. Ibid., p. 69 (quotation), pp. 69–71 (discussion).

10. Ibid., pp. 112–17; Loewy, "Duties, Fears and Physicians," p. 1364; Abigail Zuger and Steven H. Miles, "Physicians, AIDS, and Occupational Risk," *Journal of the American Medical Association* 258 (1987): 1924–25.

11. Sigerist, *Civilization and Disease*, pp. 115–16; Loewy, "Duties, Fears and Physicians," p. 1364; Geoffrey Marks, *The Medieval Plague* (Garden City, N.Y.: Doubleday, 1971); Johannes Nohl, *The Black Death* (New York: Harper, 1924).

12. Quoted in Guenter B. Risse, "Epidemics and History: Ecological Perspectives and Social Responses," in *AIDS: The Burdens of History*, ed. Elizabeth Fee and Daniel M. Fox (Berkeley: The University of California Press, 1988), p. 46.

13. The above discussion of cholera is based on ibid., pp. 40–48; and Charles E. Rosenberg, *The Cholera Years: The United States in 1832, 1849 and 1866* (Chicago: The University of Chicago Press, 1962).

14. Risse, "Epidemics and History," pp. 48–56.

15. Kenneth M. Ludmerer, *Genetics and American Society: A Historical Appraisal* (Baltimore: The Johns Hopkins University Press, 1972); Daniel J. Kevles, *In the Name of Eugenics: Genetics and the Uses of Human Heredity* (New York: Alfred A. Knopf, 1985).

16. Robert Proctor, *Racial Hygiene: Medicine Under the Nazis* (Cambridge, Mass.: Harvard University Press, 1988); Robert Jay Lifton, *The Nazi Doctors: Medical Killing and the Psychology of Genocide* (New York: Basic Books, 1986); Sheila Faith Weiss, *Race Hygiene and National Efficiency: The Eugenics of Vilhelm Schallmayer* (Berkeley: University of California Press, 1987); Alexander Mitscherlich and Fred Mielke, *Doctors of Infamy: The Story of the Nazi Medical Crimes*, trans. Heinz Norden (New York: Henry Schuman, 1949).

17. Oswei Temkin, "On the History of 'Morality and Syphilis,'" in *The Double Face of Janus and Other Essays in the History of Medicine*, ed. Oswei Temkin (Baltimore: The Johns Hopkins University Press, 1977), pp. 472–84 (quotation, p. 475); Sigerist, *Civilization and Disease*, pp. 75–79.

18. Temkin, "On the History of 'Morality and Syphilis,'" pp. 472–84; Sigerist, *Civilization and Disease*, pp. 75–79.

19. Allan M. Brandt, "AIDS: From Social History to Social Policy," in *AIDS*, ed. Fee and Fox, p. 151.

20. Ibid., pp. 151–52; idem, *No Magic Bullet: A Social History of Venereal Disease in the United States Since 1880* (New York: Oxford University Press, 1985).

21. Elizabeth Fee, "Sin Versus Science: Venereal Disease in Twentieth-Century Baltimore," in *AIDS*, ed. Fee and Fox, pp. 121–46.

22. David F. Musto, "Quarantine and the Problem of AIDS," *The Milbank Quarterly* 64, supp. 1 (1986): 110.

23. Ibid.; idem, *The American Disease: Origins of Narcotic Control* (New Haven: Yale University Press, 1973).

24. Zuger and Miles, "Physicians, AIDS, and Occupational Risk"; Loewy, "Duties, Fears and Physicians." It should not be assumed that physicians who abandoned patients were necessarily violating prevailing ethical norms. For example, the Greeks considered it unethical to attend hopeless cases; other cultures emphasized doctors' rights to accept or reject patients as they wished. Some doctors followed their patients and families into temporary exile; in other

instances doctors were threatened with physical violence by angry families and neighbors.

25. Daniel M. Fox, "The Politics of Physicians' Social Responsibility in Epidemics: A Note on History," *Hastings Center Report* 18 (April/May 1988): 5–10.

3

AIDS, the Public,
and the "NIMBY" Syndrome

Robert J. Blendon and Karen Donelan

On December 2, 1988, then–Surgeon General C. Everett Koop startled
a national audience of AIDS health professionals by proposing that it
was time for them to make their response to this dread epidemic part
of their broader public concerns about U.S. health-care problems as a
whole and to respond to this disease as they respond to other serious
illnesses.[1] To those involved in efforts to understand, treat, and control
AIDS, this statement immediately raised the question of whether the
specific problems they encounter in the care of AIDS patients through
the course of their disease are the same as those they face in the care
of people with other severe illnesses, such as cancer, heart disease, and
congenital deformities. The answer to this question has enormous implications for America's health-care system as it struggles to staff, organize,
and finance the care of more than 170,000 people projected to be living
with AIDS in 1991.[2]

This chapter seeks to provide insight into some facets of the answer
to this question. Through an in-depth examination of the views held
by the public and by health professionals toward those who have AIDS
or non-symptomatic HIV infection, we hope to help health professionals
and policymakers better understand how our society is responding to
this epidemic. Though we do not attempt to provide any comparisons
between AIDS and other illnesses with respect to specifics of clinical
and research efforts, we do offer a framework for measuring our society's
human response to a disease that is communicable and fatal and that
disproportionately affects individuals with life-styles that are considered
objectionable and are condemned by many.

In a 1988 paper presented in the *New England Journal of Medicine*,
we assessed the implications of public opinion about AIDS for the debate

over the nation's need for new anti-discrimination legislation to protect people with the disease.[3] Such legislation had been endorsed by the Presidential Commission on AIDS and the Institute of Medicine/National Academy of Sciences Committee for the Oversight of AIDS Activities chaired by Theodore Cooper, former assistant secretary for health.[2,4] In this chapter, we update and extend that analysis by including a review of more recent surveys and published studies that analyze the views of health professionals toward AIDS patients. We also consider in more depth the impact these public and professional opinions will have on the health care of AIDS patients and on the formation of public policies that will shape that care in the future.

The Public's Perspective

What are the views of the American public about AIDS and those it affects? It is important to examine them closely, for the answer to the question of whether AIDS should be viewed like other serious illnesses must be built around the realities of these opinions.

Reality 1: Americans with AIDS will likely face discrimination from a substantial segment of the population.

People who contract HIV face a double set of concerns. In addition to confronting the very serious nature of their disease, they need to consider a second concern that may be unique to this disease: the perception of 62 percent of the American public that increased testing for AIDS will lead to discrimination against those who are found to have the disease.[5] Fifty-four percent say that the epidemic has already set off a wave of anti-gay sentiment, and 48 percent say that it is leading to unfair discrimination against homosexuals.[6,7] Approximately 11 percent nationally and 17 percent among persons ages 18–29 admit that they are already trying to reduce their risk of contracting the disease by making efforts to avoid interaction with homosexuals.[8] In addition, the public sees discriminatory practices in the actions taken by government officials and political leaders. Fifty-two percent of Americans believe that the government would be spending more for AIDS research today if the disease did not disproportionately affect homosexual men.[9] An almost identical proportion (54 percent) of the population of Great Britain similarly assesses its government's slow response.[10] In both countries, providing public assistance to those with controversial life-styles remains a major political issue.

Reality 2: Those with AIDS may face loss of personal privacy and, possibly, restrictions on their civil rights.

The overwhelming majority of the public (81 percent) believes that controlling the spread of AIDS should take precedence over individual privacy; 74 percent believe that identifying those who are infected with HIV should take precedence over privacy concerns.[11,12] However, Americans are divided over whether civil liberties need to be suspended to slow the spread of the disease. Forty-two percent think such action may be necessary, and 38 percent say they would be more likely to vote for a candidate who supports strict laws against persons engaging in high-risk sexual activity.[6,13] However, 38 percent do not favor such action and 35 percent would be less likely to support a candidate who did.[6,13] There is a strong consensus for restricting the rights of individuals who may present a broader public health danger: Eighty-four percent now favor the enactment of a law that makes it a crime for a person with AIDS to donate blood; and 68 percent favor making it a criminal offense for someone who knows he or she has AIDS to have sex with another person. Support for both these measures appears to be rising when compared to the responses in 1985 of 77 percent and 51 percent, respectively.[6,13]

This level of support for measures to control the epidemic may result in increasing numbers of legislative proposals, such as the recently defeated referendum in California, that was aimed at restricting the sexual activity of infected individuals or requiring the disclosure of sexual contacts to public health departments.[14]

Reality 3: People with AIDS may confront a significant minority of Americans who show signs of intolerance and outright hostility toward them.

A series of probing survey questions elicited responses from a minority of Americans that reflect callous feelings toward people with AIDS. For example, one in four or five Americans (18 percent) candidly admits feeling no sympathy for those who have contracted AIDS as a result of homosexual activity; 23 percent have no sympathy for those infected as a result of sharing needles while using illegal drugs.[15] Similarly, one in five says that patients with AIDS are "offenders" getting what they deserve.[6] Twenty-nine percent (a figure that has doubled from 15 percent in 1985) say they favor tattooing persons who test positive for HIV.[6,13] Seventeen percent respond that those with AIDS should be sent to far-off islands as those with leprosy were in an earlier era.[11] And 75 percent would bar HIV-infected foreign visitors from the United States.[11] One in twelve Americans (one in nine with less than a high school education) says that those afflicted with the illness should not be treated with compassion.[16]

Reality 4: Patients with AIDS face a significant risk of losing their jobs and, consequently, their health insurance.

These surveys suggest a paradox. Today, only 11 percent of Americans say that working near someone is a likely way to transmit AIDS.[17] This figure has declined by more than two-thirds since 1985, when it was 37 percent.[11] However, many Americans remain apprehensive about being close to someone with AIDS in the workplace. One in four would refuse to work beside a person with AIDS, and the same proportion believes employers should have the right to fire a person just for having AIDS.[18] In the South, one in three expresses these negative attitudes.[16] The degree of potential hostility not only increases in certain regions of the country but in certain professions as well. Thirty-nine percent of Americans believe that public school employees should be dismissed if they are found to be HIV infected.[12] Forty-four percent believe that homosexuals should not be allowed to be physicians.[19]

Workplace fears of AIDS are not exclusive to the culture of this country. The proportion of people of other nationalities stating that they would refuse to work next to someone with AIDS is 68 percent in Japan and 24 percent in Canada. However, a number of countries, such as Great Britain (14 percent), Sweden (12 percent), and France (16 percent), have been more successful in reducing employee anxieties.[18]

The possible loss of employment presents an additional concern. People with AIDS also face the threat of losing their health insurance. In the United States, health insurance is largely employment-based. Eight out of ten people in the workforce obtain their health insurance coverage from their employers.[20] When someone with AIDS loses a job, Medicaid will not always provide needed assistance. Only one-half of low-income Americans are now covered by Medicaid. In some states this figure is as low as one-fifth. Clearly, in states where there is little public sympathy for those who have contracted the virus, governmental health assistance is less likely to be available than in more supportive communities.

Reality 5: Children with AIDS face the possibility that their classmates will be removed from school by parents who are anxious about exposure to HIV.

Surveys conducted since 1985 portray a change in the views of Americans about children with AIDS going to school. At that time 39 percent thought children with the disease should be barred from attendance.[21] Today only 18 percent agree.[22] There has, however, been an increase in the percentage of people who say they would keep their own child out of school to avoid contact with a student with AIDS. In 1985, this figure was 26 percent; by 1987 it had risen to 32 percent.[9,11] This will make it extremely difficult to place HIV-infected children securely in many school environments.

It seems that improved knowledge about the transmission of disease does not reassure some segments of the public. Only 10 percent (a decline from 31 percent in 1985) of the public now believe that children can contract AIDS by sitting in a classroom with someone who has the disease.[23,24] However, in contrast to the workplace, where removing the infected individual is the favored course of action, one in three parents would express anxiety about the potential danger by withdrawing his or her own child from school.[11]

Reality 6: People with AIDS face the risk of losing their housing or not having accommodations available when they require new living arrangements.

Despite the fact that 88 percent of Americans believe that they are not at increased risk of contracting AIDS by living near a hospital or home for AIDS patients, many remain apprehensive about having those with the disease residing in their communities.[24] A significant minority of the public (40 percent) say they would be upset if an AIDS patient treatment or housing center were located in their neighborhood.[11] This figure remains nearly unchanged since 1985 (44 percent).[9] Depending on the exact wording of the survey question, a substantial minority (21 percent to 40 percent) of the public favors isolating people with AIDS from the general community, public places, and their neighborhoods.[16,25] Though it is unlikely that Americans understand the full implications of quarantining the more than one million people who are estimated to be infected with HIV, 30 percent of the public express support for this policy.[5,26,27] Seventeen percent support a landlord's right to be able to evict those with the disease from their homes.[17]

When viewed as a whole, such negative public attitudes create a series of dilemmas for health professionals, public health officials, social workers, and loved ones who care for people with AIDS. Nationally, this problem of hostile attitudes has been described as the "NIMBY" (not in my backyard) syndrome. An extreme case involves individuals in New York who allegedly set fire to a foster home for infants with AIDS.[28] More commonly, it involves the eviction of people with AIDS from their apartments and neighborhood opposition to the placement of group homes for those requiring supportive care.

We do not know if these behaviors and the hostile attitudes we have described are a result of underlying dislike for the life-styles of homosexuals and IV drug users, underlying fears about the potential contagion of AIDS, or a combination of these factors. It is clear, however, that education about the transmission of the virus has not reached everyone. Despite scientific evidence to the contrary, a substantial number of people still believe that AIDS can be contracted by being coughed at or sneezed on (24 percent), by sharing drinking glasses or plates (25 percent), from public toilets (16 percent), or by sharing a telephone (12 percent).[11,24] Consequently, though few people believe that they can get AIDS simply by being next to an infected individual, many people still feel that other more specific behaviors entail a measure of risk that is unacceptable.

It is difficult to know whether additional efforts to educate the public will change these beliefs and attitudes. One example of such an effort is the recent mass mailing to 107 million homes of the surgeon general's brochure "Understanding AIDS." By all measures this would be considered a major public health education success, having elicited about 250,000 phone calls to a special educational hotline. However, nearly half of adult Americans said they did not read the report, either because they did not receive it (29 percent) or because they chose not to read it when it arrived (16 percent). Only 19 percent said they read any part of the brochure carefully.[29,30] It is clear that innovative programs are needed to reach those segments of the public that may not be accessible through conventional approaches.

The Health-Care Perspective

Given what we know about the perceptions the general public holds toward people with AIDS, what are the realities of the health-care setting for people with AIDS who seek medical care? What do we expect of our hospitals and health-care providers, and what are their feelings about caring for people affected by the epidemic? Will health professionals treat AIDS patients differently from others with serious illness?

Reality 7: AIDS patients are at risk of encountering health professionals and workers who will refuse to treat or care for them.

Americans are overwhelmingly opposed to discrimination in access to hospital care for AIDS patients (87 percent).[23] Recent incidents of health institutions turning away patients with AIDS are not acceptable to the public.[31]

However, the public is sensitive to the risks faced by health-care workers in caring for AIDS patients. Most (74 percent) support mandatory AIDS testing for those admitted to hospitals.[32] The majority (69 percent) feels that health professionals should be warned if they are asked to treat someone who has tested positive for HIV infection, and one-third (32 percent) would allow physicians to make their own choices about treating patients with the disease.[7,11] Thus, the public has more tolerance for discrimination by individual professionals in patient-care settings than by health-care institutions. This may create an environment that encourages some health professionals to avoid caring for AIDS patients.

Unfortunately, there have been very few studies published that tell us about the attitudes of health-care personnel toward caring for patients with AIDS. Those that have been done are focused on limited geographic areas and include very small samples of respondents. There are no national surveys, such as those we used to assess the attitudes of the general public. The limited information we do have tells us something that probably should not be surprising: Health-care professionals express many of the same fears and prejudices as the rest of the public. Those fears exist, at least for some physicians, in the context of increased personal risk. Though there have been very few reported cases of transmission of HIV in the health-care setting, 36 percent of medical residents surveyed in several New York hospitals reported needlestick exposures to HIV while caring for infected patients.[33] Based on a recent report by the Centers for Disease Control (CDC), the Cooperative Needlestick Surveillance Group estimates that 1 in 250 of those stuck are likely to become seropositive.[34]

Several studies highlight negative attitudes on the part of physicians toward individuals with AIDS and, in particular, toward homosexuals. In a Minnesota study of primary care physicians, 27 percent of respondents reported discomfort when treating homosexual patients, and the same proportion agreed with the statement that "homosexual behavior is not acceptable for our society." In addition, a small minority (12 percent) felt that people who contract AIDS through unconventional sexual behavior deserve their disease.[35] University of Mississippi researchers report that in a survey of their medical students, and in a similar study of physicians in Ohio, Arizona, and Tennessee, harsh attitudes were reported toward AIDS patients and homosexuals. In both studies attitudes of physicians and medical students toward patients with leukemia were contrasted with attitudes toward those with AIDS. Physicians and students considered AIDS patients to be more responsible for their illness, less deserving of sympathy and understanding, and less safe to work with in the same office.[36,37] Similarly, in a study of New York City interns and residents, one in four expressed reservations about treating patients with AIDS. The same proportion reported that they would not continue to take care of AIDS patients if given a choice. Thirty-six percent of medical house officers (19 percent pediatric) said their experience with

AIDS patients has led them to plan a career path less likely to involve the care of AIDS patients.[33]

Concerns about coming in contact with HIV patients have been voiced by non-professional hospital workers as well. One survey of hospital workers indicates that one in three employees felt that he or she should be able to refuse to care for patients with AIDS and that only 16 percent would volunteer to work with such patients.[38]

In the health-care setting, as in the general public, we cannot be certain whether more contact with individuals with AIDS will lead to less or more concern for these patients.

Reality 8: The special problems facing people with AIDS are not well understood by many Americans or health professionals.

Even though the public now sees AIDS as the most important health problem facing the country (68 percent),[16] and 86 percent report having read or heard something about the disease in the past month, most people do not feel personally affected by the epidemic: The overwhelming majority (88 percent) say they do not know someone who has or has had the disease, nor have they seen its tragic impact on a friend or family member.[24] Ninety-five percent say their chances of having or getting the AIDS virus are "low" or "none."[17] Only 20 percent of Americans report they are very concerned about getting the disease.[16,39,40] (Not all surveys show as high a level of public concern about contracting AIDS. One 1987 opinion poll reported only 6 percent of Americans were "very worried" about their own risk.[39] The larger 20 percent figure is utilized here because it is part of a continuing survey series and over time will provide a historical trend.)

Similarly, physicians have varying experiences, dependent on geographical location, in treating AIDS patients. This can be seen in the extreme difference in responses to the two physician surveys. The New York study noted that among medical interns and residents in New York City, the care of AIDS patients represented 20–25 percent of their total in-patient responsibilities.[33] The Minnesota study found that 65 percent of primary care physicians in the state had never treated an HIV-infected patient; another 23 percent had treated only one or two.[35]

Conclusions and Recommendations

What implications do these findings have for the development and implementation of policy in our communities and hospitals? The realities portrayed here suggest that AIDS will prove itself to be more than just another serious illness facing America's health-care system. The disease has a number of characteristics that make it unique in modern society. It is a disease that has disproportionately affected individuals who have life-styles that many Americans find objectionable; it is a communicable disease; and though there are treatments for episodic infections, there is no known cure for HIV. Perhaps as a result of these and other factors, disclosure of a diagnosis of HIV infection exposes individuals to discriminatory and hostile behavior from substantial numbers of the American public and health workers. Between one in four and one in five people would restrict presence in the workplace, school attendance, and neighborhood residency for those with AIDS. From smaller scale studies we see that a similar proportion of physicians and other health workers is resistant to treating AIDS patients and expresses considerable prejudicial attitudes toward their behavior and life-styles. In addition, because there is no comprehensive barrier to workplace discrimination at this time, people with AIDS are at high risk of losing their health insurance; the result would be a growing uncompensated care problem for the community at large.

It is difficult to predict whether and how public and professional attitudes will change as the epidemic goes on. One possibility is that the increased prevalence of the disease will lead to greater tolerance as more Americans are personally affected and more health professionals come in contact with patients. It is also possible, however, that as the perception of personal danger increases, hostility and discriminatory practices will increase in our society and in the health-care setting. In either case, these data provide health-care workers with perspective on the realities of the environment in which people with AIDS live, work, and obtain medical care.

At this time, those who are tested for HIV are at a substantial risk unless strict federal legislative measures are taken to guarantee the confidentiality of test results and protection from discrimination for HIV-infected people. Every effort must be made to impress upon health-care workers that there is a special importance in maintaining the confidentiality of medical information. Those who believe that this epidemic will be controlled by means of widespread voluntary testing must realize that many will be reluctant to be tested until we can assure them that they will not lose their jobs, their health insurance, and their homes if they are found to be HIV infected.

Though educational efforts have improved awareness about AIDS in the medical community, measures beyond more education are clearly required. Leaders in the health professions and in hospitals need to establish a series of strictly enforced guidelines to define, encourage, and enforce ethical behavior in the care of AIDS patients. Prior research has shown that established institutional norms can alter prejudicial and discriminatory behavior in various settings, even if discriminatory attitudes persist.[41,42]

Implemented together, these recommendations would create an environment in which physicians, nurses, and other health-care workers can more appropriately and sensitively care for those infected with HIV.

Methods

The data reported in this chapter come from a review of 60 national and international opinion surveys, including over 800 questions, conducted between 1983 and 1988. These surveys were undertaken by 14 national survey organizations and the National Center for Health Statistics (NCHS), using different research methods and instruments. Nearly every survey cited involved telephone or personal interviews of between 1,000 and 5,000 randomly selected adults. Surveys by ABC News in 1987 and Gordon Black/*USA Today* in 1988 had smaller samples. NCHS conducted household interviews in person with over 17,000 people between August and December 1987, and an additional 7,253 people in May and June 1988.

When one interprets these findings, it should be recognized that all such surveys are subject to sampling error. Results may differ, therefore, from what would be obtained if the whole population were interviewed. The size of these errors varies with the number of people in each survey. The sampling error for a survey of 1,000 respondents is estimated at ±4 percent for each question.

Responses from telephone surveys tend to underrepresent slightly the views of some members of the population, particularly individuals of low income. During the survey period, an estimated 5 to 7 percent of households in the United States were without telephone service and were, therefore, excluded from these surveys.

In addition, the chapter includes data from six published studies of the attitudes of health professionals and workers toward those with AIDS. There are limitations to the interpretations of these studies. None are national in scope, unlike the public opinion surveys. Numbers of respondents are much smaller. They are all restricted to particular geographic locations that may not be comparable because of varying incidence of HIV infection, particular social norms, or other factors unknown to the authors.

Notes

1. C.E. Koop, Conference on "Hospitals, Health Care Professionals and AIDS," December 1–2, 1988, Boston, Mass.

2. National Academy of Sciences, *Confronting AIDS: Update 1988* (Washington, D.C.: National Academy Press, 1988).

3. R.J. Blendon and K. Donelan, "Discrimination Against People with AIDS: The Public's Perspective," *New England Journal of Medicine* 319 (1988): 1022–26.

4. *Report of the Presidential Commission on the Human Immunodeficiency Virus Epidemic, June 24, 1988* (Washington, D.C.: U.S. Government Printing Office, 0-214-701, 1988).

5. ABC News, June 1987 (Storrs, Conn.: Roper Center for Public Opinion Research).

6. *Los Angeles Times,* July 28, 1987 (Storrs, Conn.: Roper Center for Public Opinion Research).

7. Gallup/*Newsweek,* November 24, 1986 (Storrs, Conn.: Roper Center for Public Opinion Research).

8. The Gallup Poll, "Knowledge of AIDS Is Widespread; Many Taking Preventative Measures," November 27, 1988.

9. ABC News/*Washington Post,* September 1985 (Storrs, Conn.: Roper Center for Public Opinion Research).

10. Social Surveys Ltd. (Gallup Poll), August 1986, in *Index to International Public Opinion 1986–1987,* ed. E.H. Hastings and P.K. Hastings (New York: Greenwood Press, 1988), p. 192.

11. Louis Harris and Associates, "AIDS Survey," August 1987 (Storrs, Conn.: Roper Center for Public Opinion Research).

12. ABC News/*Washington Post,* March 11, 1987 (Storrs, Conn.: Roper Center for Public Opinion Research).

13. *Los Angeles Times,* December 1985 (Storrs, Conn.: Roper Center for Public Opinion Research).

14. D. Pence, "The AIDS Epidemic: Paradox and Purpose in Public Health Policy," *Vital Speeches* 54 (1988): 252–56.

15. CBS News/*New York Times* Poll, "AIDS and Intravenous Drug Use," September 8–11, 1988.

16. "AIDS: America's Most Important Health Problem," *The Gallup Report,* Nos. 268/269, January/February 1988.

17. The Gallup Poll, November 22, 1987 (Storrs, Conn.: Roper Center for Public Opinion Research).

18. "AIDS: 35-Nation Survey," *The Gallup Report,* No. 273, June 1988.

19. The Gallup Poll, March 18, 1987 (Storrs, Conn.: Roper Center for Public Opinion Research).

20. Congressional Research Service, *Health Insurance and the Uninsured: Background Data and Analysis,* Special Committee on Aging Serial 100-I (Washington, D.C.: U.S. Government Printing Office, 1988).

21. NBC News, November 20, 1985 (Storrs, Conn.: Roper Center for Public Opinion Research).

22. Tarrance/Survey Research International, "Health Care Issues," April 1988 (Storrs, Conn.: Roper Center for Public Opinion Research).

23. Louis Harris and Associates, "Harris Survey," September 23, 1985 (Storrs, Conn.: Roper Center for Public Opinion Research).

24. D.A. Dawson, M. Cynamon, and J.E. Fitti, National Center for Health Statistics, *AIDS Knowledge and Attitudes, Provisional Data from the National Health Interview Survey: United States,* September 1987. Advance data from Vital and Health Statistics, No. 147, Department of Health and Human Services Pub. No. (PHS) 88-1250 (Hyattsville, Md.: Public Health Service, 1987).

25. Gallup Organization/*Times Mirror,* "The People, the Press and Politics," September 1987 (Storrs, Conn.: Roper Center for Public Opinion Research).

26. Centers for Disease Control, "Human Immunodeficiency Virus Infection in the United States: A Review of Current Knowledge," *Morbidity and Mortality Weekly Report* 36, supp. 6 (1987): 1–48.

27. D.F. Musto, "Quarantine and the Problem of AIDS," *The Milbank Quarterly* 64, supp. 1 (1986): 97–117.

28. M. Hornblower, "Not in My Backyard You Don't," *Time,* June 27, 1988, pp. 44–45.

29. The Gallup Poll, July 20, 1988, Los Angeles Times Syndicate.

30. D.A. Dawson, *AIDS Knowledge and Attitudes for July 1988.* Advance data from Vital and Health Statistics, No. 161, Department of Health and Human Services Pub. No. (PHS) 89-1250 (Hyattsville, Md.: Public Health Service, 1988).

31. "Two Facilities to Refuse AIDS Virus Carriers," *The Boston Globe,* June 25, 1988, p. 16.

32. Roper Organization/*U.S. News and World Report*/CNN, April 1, 1987 (Storrs, Conn.: Roper Center for Public Opinion Research).

33. R.N. Link et al., "Concerns of Medical and Pediatric House Officers About Acquiring AIDS from Their Patients," *American Journal of Public Health* 78 (1988): 455–59.

34. R. Marcus, "Surveillance of Health Care Workers Exposed to Blood from Patients Infected with the Human Immunodeficiency Virus," *New England Journal of Medicine* 319 (1988): 1118–23.

35. J.M. Shultz et al., "The Minnesota AIDS Physician Survey: A Statewide Survey of Physician Knowledge and Clinical Practice Regarding AIDS," *Minnesota Medicine* 71 (1988): 277–83.

36. J.A. Kelly et al., "Medical Students' Attitudes Toward AIDS and Homosexual Patients," *Journal of Medical Education* 62 (1987): 549–56.

37. J.A. Kelly et al., "Stigmatization of AIDS Patients by Physicians," *American Journal of Public Health* 77 (1987): 789–91.

38. F.M. Gordin et al., "Knowledge of AIDS Among Hospital Workers: Behavioral Correlates and Consequences," *AIDS* 1 (1987): 183–88.

39. H. Quinley, "The New Facts of Life: Heterosexuals and AIDS," *Public Opinion,* May/June 1988, pp. 53–55.

40. Gordon Black/*USA Today,* June 7, 1988 (Storrs, Conn.: Roper Center for Public Opinion Research).

41. S.J. Gross and C.M. Niman, "Attitude-Behavior Consistency: A Review," *Public Opinion Quarterly* 39 (1975): 358–68.

42. B. Kutner, C. Wilkins, and P.R. Yarrow, "Verbal Attitudes and Overt Behavior Involving Racial Prejudice," *Journal of Abnormal Social Psychology* 47 (1952): 649–52.

4

Physicians' Attitudes Toward AIDS

M. Roy Schwarz

Few would disagree that AIDS has presented medicine and physicians with the most complex set of challenges since the polio and typhoid epidemics of the first half of the twentieth century. Not only has the biology of the disease posed vexing problems for the profession, but the ethical dilemmas have confounded even the most thoughtful physicians and have resulted in deep divisions among them.

This chapter provides an overview of the attitudes of physicians toward AIDS. The discussion largely reflects the results of surveys conducted by the American Medical Association (AMA) from 1987 to 1989.[1,2,3] Comparisons are also made with other studies of physicians' attitudes, including some studies from Great Britain.

Homophobia

The AMA has not conducted surveys specifically about the attitudes of physicians toward homosexuals, but several reports that provide some insights have been published. In a survey of Minnesota physicians, 81 percent of whom were heterosexuals, one in five (21 percent) admitted to having "moderate or great discomfort" in dealing with homosexual patients.[4] Twenty-seven percent believed that the homosexual life-style is (or should be) unacceptable to society, and 35 percent believed that the homosexual life-style should be condemned. These negative feelings were much more common to physicians who had little or no contact with AIDS patients than to those who had treated sizable numbers of AIDS patients.

In a three-city study, over 500 physicians were asked to read and answer questions about vignettes comparing patients with leukemia and AIDS.[5] The most strongly held view of the study was that AIDS patients were responsible for their own illness. Many physicians felt that AIDS patients deserved to be ill, that they were dangerous to others, and that they should be quarantined. Compared to leukemia patients, AIDS patients fared poorly in physicians' willingness to attend parties with them (regardless of whether food was being prepared by AIDS patients), to work in the same office with them, or to allow their own children to visit them.

Two small studies comparing the attitudes of physicians and nurses in New York City in 1983 and 1986 reported that one-third of the physicians surveyed had negative feelings toward homosexuals in both years.[6,7,8] In contrast, the percentage of nurses who felt negatively decreased from 30 percent to 15 percent over this three-year period. In another study that involved physicians in California, including San Francisco and Los Angeles, one-third admitted a "moderate amount or a good deal of discomfort" in dealing with AIDS patients who are gay.[9]

Finally, in a study involving physicians belonging to the Los Angeles County Medical Association (LACMA) and/or the Southern California Physicians for Human Rights (SCPHR), 21 percent of the physicians believed, either strongly or moderately, that gays brought the disease upon themselves.[10] Thirty-five percent were angry at the threat that AIDS poses for "straights," and 41 percent were less accepting of the gay life-style as a result of the epidemic than they were before AIDS appeared. In this study, fewer of the physicians belonging to the SCPHR felt this way than did those belonging to LACMA. These results were similar to the study of another California medical society, reported in the *Western Journal of Medicine* in 1986.[11]

In summary, it appears that about one-third of physicians hold negative views of homosexual life-styles. This group believes that the gay community has brought the AIDS epidemic upon itself and that it deserves the result. These views, no doubt, color all their other attitudes about the disease.

Fear

The issue of fear among physicians in the face of epidemics is not new. Thomas Sydenham in the seventeenth century, like Galen in the second, fled from the Black Plague. In contrast, Guy de Chauliac, physician to the Pope and a noted surgeon in the fourteenth century, continued to practice in spite of his fear.[12] It is difficult to isolate the issue of fear in relation to AIDS because it is intertwined with homophobia, family and staff concerns, goals for treating AIDS patients, and the presence or absence of children.

In one of the AMA's surveys, physicians were asked whether they were concerned about accidentally contracting AIDS: 15 percent answered "very," 40 percent "somewhat," 23 percent "not very," and 20 percent indicated "not at all."[1] Sixty-three percent of the physicians admitted that their families would be concerned if they increased the number of AIDS patients they were treating, and 70 percent believed that their staff would be concerned under the same circumstances.

In a study of physicians who work with AIDS patients in San Francisco, of whom 33 percent were heterosexual and 67 percent homosexual, the following percentages expressed that they experienced "much more" of each feeling after they began to deal with AIDS patients: fear (46 percent), depression (36 percent), anxiety (44 percent), overwork (39 percent), and stress (56 percent). Gay physicians experienced these feelings more severely than did the non-gay physicians, and all physicians expressed much more career satisfaction and intellectual stimulation after they started to treat AIDS patients.[13]

Of special interest is the impact that fear of AIDS may be having on housestaff training. A recent study revealed that 48 percent of medical and 30 percent of pediatric housestaff in seven New York City hospitals had "moderate to major concern" over contracting the disease.[14] Concern was greater in newer residents and in those caring for increasing numbers of AIDS patients. Twenty-five percent would not treat AIDS patients if they had a choice; 36 percent of the medical residents and 90 percent of the pediatric residents would choose career paths in which they would encounter fewer AIDS patients. The fear of AIDS patients, however, had no influence on their choices of residency, and more than three-quarters were moderately or not at all resentful of having to care for AIDS patients. Resuscitation and intensive care of AIDS patients, however, made residents very uncomfortable and posed, in their minds, very serious ethical dilemmas.[15,16]

It is important to note that other factors, including AIDS caseloads, the intensity of the care that AIDS patients required, the poor prognosis for people with AIDS, the limitations of technology, and the constant necessity of dealing with death, undoubtedly contributed to the residents' attitudes.

Not surprisingly, fear is a significant component of their feelings as physicians try to deal with the AIDS epidemic. To what extent this influences their opinions is impossible to quantify. It is reasonable to assume, however, that fear influences physicians' opinions to a major degree on such issues as gay life-styles, testing, reporting, contact tracing, and the obligation to treat AIDS patients. It would be infinitely more valuable to recognize the presence of the fear and deal with it directly than to deny its existence.

Mandatory Reporting

Among the most vexing challenges of AIDS is the issue of reporting the disease or serostatus of an individual to public health authorities. Public debate rages over the right and the need to protect society and uninfected individuals. Fueled by concerns over egregious examples of discrimination and the fear that discrimination will drive the high-risk population underground, thus thwarting attempts to control the epidemic, the issue of mandatory reporting has occupied endless hours of public policy debate.

When 500 physicians (in family medicine, internal medicine, pediatrics, and obstetrics/gynecology) were queried about this issue, 47 percent indicated that they were in favor of reporting all seropositive patients to public health authorities.[1] Another 34 percent favored reporting patients with AIDS or AIDS-related complex (ARC). Since these patients would also be seropositive, a total of 81 percent apparently favored reporting seropositive patients. Thirteen percent did not want anyone reported, even those with the disease. Physicians who had treated a significant number of AIDS patients and physicians from the middle Atlantic region of the country were more opposed to mandatory reporting than were physicians at large. We can compare these results with those of the sample of physicians in Minnesota, of whom 93 percent favored reporting AIDS cases, 87 percent favored reporting ARC cases, and 71 percent were in favor of reporting seropositivity in the absence of any symptoms.[4] In contrast, only 36 percent of general practitioners in the Northwest Thames and East Anglian regions of Great Britain favored seropositive status reporting.[17]

Contact Tracing

Equally as explosive as the issue of reporting seropositivity is the issue of contact tracing. In one of the AMA studies, 80 percent of physicians supported contact tracing of AIDS patients by public health authorities.[1] Sixty-three percent also supported tracing by any means available of all patients who are seropositive. This number dropped to 60 percent for physicians who have treated over five AIDS patients. Further division of opinion was noted when physicians were asked if they should break confidentiality to inform a sexual partner of an infected person when the infected person refused to do so. Forty-three percent indicated they would break confidentiality and 45 percent said they would not.

The Minnesota study reported that 81 percent of physicians favored patient-initiated contact tracing and 76 percent favored health department contact tracing.[4] In a study of Michigan physicians' attitudes, 91 percent of surgeons and 86 percent of non-surgeons believed that health authorities should conduct contact tracing and notification programs.[18]

It appears, therefore, that the majority of physicians are in favor of contact tracing but differ on who should conduct the tracing.

HIV-Positive Physicians

Increasing debate has occurred in medical and public circles over the issue of the rights, responsibilities, and roles of a physician who has AIDS or who has tested positive for AIDS. In one of the AMA studies, when asked if HIV-positive physicians are obligated to inform patients and co-workers of their condition, 48 percent responded affirmatively, 39 percent were opposed, and 12 percent were uncertain.[1] Physicians experienced with AIDS were more opposed, and obstetricians and gynecologists were more in favor than were internists.

When asked whether HIV-positive physicians should continue to see patients and, if so, under what circumstances, 50 percent felt treatment should continue but only for non-invasive procedures. Twenty-eight percent felt full or unlimited practice could continue if CDC-recommended precautions were adhered to. Eleven percent thought practice should continue without restrictions, and 9 percent thought all practice should be discontinued. Physicians experienced with AIDS were more likely to differentiate between invasive and non-invasive procedures when expressing their opinions.

In another study, Michigan physicians were asked whether physicians should be tested for HIV infection.[18] Sixty-two percent of surgeons and 47 percent of non-surgeons answered yes.

Pre-Admission HIV Testing

Another troublesome ethical issue facing physicians is whether pre-admission HIV testing should be mandatory for patients entering the hospital, especially those patients who will undergo surgical procedures. While the public rhetoric has been very intense on the issue of mandatory testing of patients, especially those who are to be hospitalized, few comprehensive studies have been conducted of physicians' attitudes on this matter. In a report from Great Britain, between 80 and 91 percent of physicians in various specialties felt all homosexuals, IV drug abusers, and hemophiliacs should be screened prior to admission to the hospital. In contrast, only 11 to 24 percent (including 10 percent of surgeons) felt all patients entering a hospital should be screened.[19]

The AMA House of Delegates believes that all blood donors, tissue donors (including sperm), immigrants, military recruits, and prisoners should be routinely tested on a mandatory basis. With regard to hospital pre-admission screening, the posture is to leave this issue to local option. It is believed that some hospitals in high-risk areas may be justified in instituting mandatory screening but that such a posture is not applicable to all hospitals.[20]

Obligations to Treat AIDS Patients

Sound evidence exists that physicians have, during the great contagious plagues of history, continued to treat afflicted patients, often at great peril to their own lives. Hippocrates, Procopius, Guy de Chauliac, Gentile da Foligno, Thomas Wharton, Francis Glisson, and Benjamin Rush, among others, stand out as noble examples of this ethical behavior.[21] With the appearance of AIDS, the issue has once again surfaced. Almost without exception, authors who have written on this subject have concluded that if physicians have the requisite medical expertise, they have an obligation to treat AIDS patients, even if they are put at great personal risk by this action.[21-28] However, the question of how physicians at large feel about this matter remains unanswered.

An unpublished report by John Rizzo, William Marder, and Richard Wilke, involving nearly 3,000 physicians across the country, maintained that 75.3 percent of the physicians queried agreed that a physician may not ethically refuse to treat a patient whose condition is within the physician's current realm of competence, solely because the patient is HIV seropositive.[3] This attitude was remarkably constant across all types of practice, years in practice, board certification, country of medical school graduation, number of AIDS patients treated, population of practice location, gender, and family situations. There was, however, significant variation by specialty. The highest degrees of agreement were in emergency medicine (89.2 percent), pediatrics (85.7 percent), general internal medicine (85.1 percent), and psychiatry (81.9 percent). The lowest degrees of agreement were in surgical sub-specialties (59 percent), obstetrics and gynecology (64 percent), anesthesia (66.2 percent), and general surgery (68.6 percent).

These results are consistent with earlier, less comprehensive studies[9,18] and suggest that the majority of physicians agree with the posture assumed by their predecessors. Physicians who are more intimately exposed to the AIDS virus (e.g., surgeons) and are at higher risk are more likely to dissent from the obligation to treat than are those who are more distant from AIDS patients. These differences are consistent with the past behavior of some physicians. Those opposed represent a distinct minority.

Medical Information

Forty-one percent of physicians queried in the AMA studies indicated that they have "a lot of information" about AIDS, while 50 percent have "a fair amount" and 8 percent have "not too much."[1,2] Eighty percent reported relying on journals as their primary source of information, and two-thirds indicated that they trusted the journals "totally" or "a great deal." Nearly 28.5 percent had "moderate trust" and 4.4 percent expressed "very little" or "no confidence" in journals. When asked if their community-based colleagues possessed the requisite knowledge to treat AIDS patients, 80 percent felt that their colleagues lacked the knowledge required for treatment. Ninety-one percent felt, however, that physicians should take the lead in providing the public with an understanding of the disease. That physicians want more information is evident from many studies.[4,10,17,19]

In a related question, when physicians were asked who should treat AIDS patients, 48 percent opted for specialists and 45 percent preferred physicians who had more universal training so that all could share the burden. The more AIDS experience physicians had, the more they tended to opt for universal care. Specifically, of physicians who had treated ten AIDS patients, 73 percent opted for universal care by all physicians.[1]

Miscellaneous Opinions

A number of other attitudes emerged in the course of the AMA studies.[1,2] Seventy-five percent of the physicians queried believed AIDS to be "a very serious health problem," while 21 percent believed it was "somewhat serious," and 3 percent "not too serious." Forty-two percent of the physicians believed that too little money was being spent for research on AIDS, while 3.4 percent felt the amount was "about right." Seventy-eight percent felt that children with AIDS should be allowed to attend regular school classes, 8 percent were opposed, and 14 percent were unsure. Sixty percent felt that a person with AIDS should continue working; 8 percent were opposed; 28 percent felt that it depends on the job; and 4 percent were unsure.

When asked to what extent they trusted the federal government to make appropriate decisions about AIDS, 44 percent replied "moderately," and 35 percent said "not at all" or "very little." Nineteen percent indicated "totally" or "very much."[1]

Analysis

It is clear from a review of the available data on physicians' attitudes that the level of knowledge about and experience with AIDS patients influence opinions. So it stands to reason that as the amount of knowledge increases, there will be a shift in attitudes. Since physicians' understanding is rapidly evolving, shifts in attitudes can be expected to occur over time. Numerous studies show that as experience in treating AIDS increases, comfort with the life-style will also increase. There will also be a shift in the intensity of feelings about reporting. This is consistent with the predominant view that all physicians should treat AIDS patients. It is also consistent with the perception that colleagues lack the information necessary to treat patients and with the opinion concerning the amount of information that individual physicians possess. One survey found that physicians would respond to a variety of learning techniques and formats.[4] All of this seems to mandate increasing emphasis on AIDS education for all physicians.

Although the degree of homophobia among surveyed physicians remains uncertain, it is clear that about one-third of the physicians have reservations about gay life-styles, including those who believe that the gay community brought the epidemic upon itself and that it deserves the consequences. These attitudes most likely influence other attitudes concerning testing, reporting, and contact tracing.

Some caution is probably called for in the interpretation of residents' attitudes. The one-fourth of residents who would not treat AIDS if they had a choice may represent fatigue from overexposure to patients with AIDS, emotional exhaustion, and/or a desire for a broader base of medical education experience. Boredom may also explain at least some of the attitudes uncovered in this review.

With regard to fear, it is not surprising that a very significant number of physicians admit that they are fearful of becoming infected through contact with seropositive or disease-bearing patients. Given the fatal nature of the disease and the apparent dearth of information possessed by physicians, it is, in a sense, surprising that the levels of fear reported were not higher. Since risk can be reduced to reasonable levels by the use of appropriate precautions, it is probable that increased availability of information—through education—will decrease fear. Some fear, or better, caution is appropriate and serves to motivate proper risk-reduction behavior. Open discussions about the issue of physician fear, including where the fear comes from, how it expresses itself, and how it can be managed, would be useful.

Attitudes about testing, reporting test results by name to health officers, contact tracing, and pre-admission testing of patients (with or without informed consent) will undoubtedly shift with time as the epidemic continues. If discrimination can be brought under control, if attitudes are similar to those during previous infectious epidemics, and if the disease is treated as an infectious disease and not as a social, political, religious, or moral disease, then, over time, more testing, reporting, and tracing will occur. Whether physicians will lead this change or follow it will be worth observing.

A number of major ethical issues remain unsettled in the minds of physicians. The most obvious of these is the issue surrounding the duty to treat. Given historical behaviors, one may conclude that the majority of physicians do now, and will in the future, remain at their posts delivering care to AIDS patients, even if their own survival is placed in jeopardy by such action. This is the only defensible posture that can be chosen if the oath that all physicians take is to have any meaning. Failure to take this posture and to behave accordingly further attenuates the already strained social contract between the medical profession and the public. The duty to treat is so fundamental to the concept of a caring profession that its absence violates the premises underlying the doctor-patient relationship and the meaning of being a physician.

What, then, is the status of the soul of the medical profession in the United States as revealed by these attitude surveys? While many answers are possible, it is safe to conclude that, in general, the profession possesses the right values and attitudes. It is clear, however, that there is also a tremendous opportunity for improvement. The latter conclusion has major implications for all aspects of medical education, including the criteria for medical school admissions, the undergraduate medical education experience, graduate training, and continuing medical education. Unfortunately, the profession has not given sufficient attention to these matters, and such attention is now being demanded by the public.

Notes

The author wishes to acknowledge the able assistance of William R. Hendee, Ph.D., John Henning, Ph.D., William D. Marder, John A. Rizzo, Ph.D., Richard J. Wilke, Ph.D., Rita M. Palulonis, Jaye D. Barr-Hill, and Charles Macenski in the preparation of this paper.

1. L.B. Bresolin et al., "Knowledge and Attitudes of Primary Care Physicians About Acquired Immunodeficiency Syndrome," unpublished data (Chicago: American Medical Association, 1989.)

2. *American Medical Association Surveys of Physician and Public Opinion on Health Care Issues* (Chicago: American Medical Association, 1988).

3. J.A. Rizzo, W.D. Marder, and R.J. Wilke, "Physician Contact with and Attitudes Toward HIV-Seropositive Patients: Results from a National Survey," (Chicago: American Medical Association, 1989), mimeo.

4. J.M. Shultz et al., "The Minnesota AIDS Physician Survey," *Minnesota Medicine* 71 (1988): 277–83.

5. J.A. Kelly et al., "Stigmatization of AIDS Patients by Physicians," *American Journal of Public Health* 77 (1987): 789–91.

6. C.J. Douglas, C.M. Kalman, and T.P. Kalman, "Homophobia Among Physicians and Nurses: An Empirical Study," *Hospital and Community Psychiatry* 36 (1985): 1309–11.

7. T.P. Kalman et al., "Homophobia Reassessed," *Hospital and Community Psychiatry* 38 (1987): 996.

8. T.P. Kalman, C.M. Kalman, and C.J. Douglas, "Homophobia Among Physicians and Nurses Treating AIDS Patients," *Hospital and Community Psychiatry* 144 (1987): 1514–15.

9. C.E. Lewis, H.D. Freeman, and C.R. Corey, "AIDS-Related Competence of California Primary Care Physicians," *American Journal of Public Health* 77 (1987): 795–99.

10. J.L. Richardson et al., "Physicians' Attitudes and Experiences Regarding the Care of Patients with Acquired Immunodeficiency Syndrome (AIDS) and Related Disorders (ARC)," *Medical Care* 25 (1987): 675–85.

11. W.C. Matthews et al., "Physician Attitudes Toward Homosexuality: Survey of a California Medical Society," *Western Journal of Medicine* 144 (1986): 106–10.

12. E.H. Loewy, "AIDS and the Physician's Fear of Contagion," *Chest* 89 (1986): 325–26.

13. L. McKusick et al., "The Psychological Impact of AIDS on Primary Care Physicians," *Western Journal of Medicine* 144 (1986): 751–52.

14. N.R. Link et al., "Concerns of Medical and Pediatric House Officers About Acquiring AIDS from Their Patients," *American Journal of Public Health* 78 (1988): 455–59.

15. R.M. Wachter et al., "Attitudes of Medical Residents Regarding Intensive Care for Patients with the Acquired Immunodeficiency Syndrome," *Archives of Internal Medicine* 148 (1988): 149–52.

16. R.M. Wachter, "The Impact of the Acquired Immunodeficiency Syndrome on Medical Resident Training," *New England Journal of Medicine* 314 (1986): 177–80.

17. R. Boyton and G. Scambler, "Survey of General Practitioners' Attitudes to AIDS in the North West Thames and East Anglian Regions," *British Medical Journal* 296 (1988): 538–40.

18. Rose B. Heald, "Physicians' Attitudes About AIDS," *Michigan Medicine* (December 1988): 763–65.

19. E.S. Searle, "Knowledge, Attitudes and Behaviour of Health Professionals in Relation to AIDS," *Lancet* 1, No. 8523 (1987): 26–28.

20. American Medical Association Proceedings, "Prevention and Control of AIDS: An Interim Report," *Report YY* of the Board of Trustees, Chicago, Illinois, June 21–25, 1987, pp. 181–93.

21. E.H. Loewy, "Duties, Fears and Physicians," *Social Science Medicine* 22 (1986): 1363–66.

22. American Medical Association Proceedings, "Ethical Issues Involved in the Growing AIDS Crisis," *Report A* of the Council on Ethical and Judicial Affairs, Chicago, Illinois, December 6–9, 1987, pp. 168–69.

23. E.J. Emmanuel, "Do Physicians Have an Obligation to Treat Patients with AIDS?" *New England Journal of Medicine* 318 (1988): 1686–90.

24. J.D. Arras, "The Fragile Web of Responsibility: AIDS and the Duty to Treat," *Hastings Center Report* (April/May 1988): 10–20.

25. G.N. Burrow, "Caring for AIDS Patients: The Physician's Risk and Responsibility," *Canadian Medical Association Journal* 129 (1983): 1181.

26. H. Frank, "AIDS: The Responsibility of Health Workers to Assume Some Degree of Personal Risk," *Western Journal of Medicine* 144 (1986): 363–64.

27. T. Smith, "AIDS: A Doctor's Duty," *British Medical Journal* 294 (1987): 6.

28. S.C. Sharp, "The Physician's Obligation to Treat AIDS Patients," *Southern Medical Journal* 81 (1988): 1282–85.

5

Nurse Attitudes and AIDS

Gayling Gee

Nurses in all disciplines and in a variety of settings are involved in the battle against human immunodeficiency virus (HIV) infection, acquired immune deficiency syndrome (AIDS), and AIDS-related conditions. Medical-surgical, critical care, emergency, psychiatric and neuroscience, maternal-child, school and public health, hospice, home care, nephrology, ophthalmology, occupational health, surgical, oncology, and enterostomal nurses each contribute to the nursing care and knowledge base of AIDS. Direct care, patient and community education, testing and counseling, research, case management and referral, emotional support, and infection control are some of the activities in which nurses are engaged. Of all the care providers, nurses spend the most time with patients. The informational and support needs of nurses in all these disciplines are great.[1]

As HIV infection and AIDS become more common, increasing numbers of nurses will be required to care for a growing population of physically and mentally frail individuals with AIDS. Earlier disease detection, the increasing incidence of associated neurologic disease, the use of anti-virals and other agents that prolong life but do not cure, and the growing numbers of infected individuals threaten to exacerbate the existing AIDS care problems. Planning for the nursing care of these patients must take place on an organized, national level. If opportunities to understand and promote nursing activities related to AIDS are ignored, the health-care crisis caused by the epidemic could accelerate further, and the social consequences of a runaway disease would be devastating.

Public Opinion

The National Academy of Sciences and the President's Commission on AIDS have both cited the fear of discrimination as a major constraint to the wide acceptance of many potentially effective public health measures.[2] In a national survey of public perspectives on AIDS discrimination, R. Blendon and K. Donelan found that 62 percent of those questioned see an increase in discrimination against people with HIV infection or AIDS, including a rise in anti-homosexual violence and harassment. Eighty-one percent agree that the control of AIDS may require the loss of individual privacy and restrictions on civil rights. Seventeen to 29 percent of those polled feel that AIDS patients are getting their rightful due, favor tattooing infected individuals, and favor treating such patients as lepers by sending them off to a distant colony; 9 percent feel that AIDS patients should not be treated with compassion. Additionally, between 18 and 39 percent of people surveyed refuse to work next to an AIDS patient, favor dismissing infected public school employees, favor barring infected children from school, and would keep their child out of school if an infected child were in attendance.

Nurses, of course, are also members of the public and are neither isolated from nor unaffected by public attitudes. Despite their education and training, nurses' perceptions on a variety of issues will be influenced both positively and negatively by their familial, cultural, and socioeconomic backgrounds. To what extent do nurses share these public attitudes? How will their decisions regarding how they will care for AIDS patients or whether they will refuse to care for someone be affected? What are these attitudes and how can they be modified so that all patients will receive positive, compassionate, non-judgmental, and quality nursing care?

Nurses in Practice

In 1984, P. Reed, T. Wise, and L. Mann revealed the results of a study surveying the attitudes of 267 nurses caring for AIDS patients (including RNs, LPNs, assistants, orderlies, and management) at a 650-bed tertiary-care hospital.[3] Of the respondents, 27.3 percent had given direct care, 9.7 percent had handled patient specimens, and 61.4 percent had no previous exposure to AIDS patients.

Results showed that more than 80 percent had a reasonable understanding of AIDS. Of the nurses surveyed, 66.7 percent expressed "some" to "quite a bit" of anxiety with regard to providing care, and 49.2 percent stated that their families had "some" to "quite a bit" of anxiety over the same issue. Approximately 25 percent of the nurses identified homosexuality as a mental/psychiatric disorder, while 65 percent viewed it as a life-style. When asked if they would refuse to work with an AIDS patient, 92.9 percent stated that they would not refuse to provide care. Fear of contagion and homophobia were expressed repeatedly by the population surveyed, and such feelings were particularly strong in the group (3 percent) who stated they would refuse to provide care.

M. Blumenfield et al. conducted surveys in 1983 and 1984 of 298 nurses in a 619-bed urban teaching hospital.[4] They found that between one-quarter and one-half of the nurses polled feared caring for male prisoners and homosexual men because of AIDS. Two-thirds of the nurses had family and friends who were concerned about their contact with AIDS patients. Approximately half of the nurses surveyed also believed that AIDS could be transmitted in the workplace during patient contact as well as by contact with patient specimens, despite the taking of precautions. Half of the nurses feared caring for an AIDS patient more than they feared caring for a hepatitis patient, and half of the nurses surveyed would also request a transfer if they had to care for AIDS patients on a regular basis.

These early studies highlighted the fears and concerns of nurses as the AIDS epidemic grew. Fear of contagion persisted despite findings that nurses were knowledgeable about AIDS and despite attendance at educational classes. Fears of homosexual male patients were strong even though a general tolerance of homosexual life-style was evident. Many nurses would not refuse to care for an AIDS patient but would prefer not to do it on a regular basis. Families and friends of nurses expressed concerns, thus putting additional pressure on nurses to avoid caring for AIDS patients.

Between 1984 and 1988, considerable educational efforts, both public and professional, were mounted in an effort to prepare nurses to care for AIDS patients. The continued rise in the number of AIDS patients exposed greater numbers of nurses to these issues.

D.C. Wertz and colleagues pre- and post-tested 1,247 care providers, 67 percent of whom were RNs, LPNs, and nursing students, to assess the impact of education on knowledge and attitudes about AIDS.[5] While knowledge about the modes of transmission and infection control improved significantly, a high percentage of respondents still believed that AIDS could be transmitted by sharing coffee cups (72 percent), by shaking hands (11 percent), and by touching toilet seats (46 percent), equipment (30 percent), bed sheets (46 percent), and doorknobs (9 percent). Attitudes about AIDS patients also shifted, with respondents expressing increased confidence in their ability to protect themselves, provide competent care, and interact with the lovers of AIDS patients. Given the choice, 18 percent would still prefer to avoid caring for persons with AIDS, and 16 percent felt hospital workers should not be required to care for AIDS patients. Interestingly, those who were responsible for establishing regulations and those who worked in the out-patient setting demonstrated greater knowledge and comfort in caring for AIDS patients than those who worked in the in-patient setting. Thus, while education proved effective in improving knowledge and attitudes, a significant amount of misinformation about modes of transmission still existed.

Two more recent surveys have been completed and provide updated information and broader nursing representation on this issue. L. Brennan polled 346 nurses nationwide, 95 percent of whom were RNs, at fifteen hospitals that were known to care for AIDS patients.[6] Concern for their own safety (73 percent) remained the major fear of the nurses. While 47 percent were frustrated by the poor prognosis of the disease, a significant percentage were also accepting (42 percent) and challenged (36 percent) by the care needs. Fear of (27 percent) and anger at (19 percent) the disease, the hospital and government, and the patients themselves were other feelings expressed. Family concerns over the nurse's safety (80 percent) and the family's own safety (32 percent) were greater than ever, and fear (36 percent) and anger (12 percent) on the family's part were as great as the nurse's. While 82 percent of the nurses had never had symptoms they considered indicative of AIDS, over 75 percent worried "sometimes" to "all the time" about getting AIDS themselves, and over one-third worried about giving it to their families. Overall, 21 percent enjoyed caring for AIDS patients while 37 percent expressed moderate to intense dislike for providing care to them. The remainder (41 percent) expressed ambivalence in how they felt, citing as causes their concern about contagion and conflict with certain life-styles. While 93 percent of the nurses had never refused to care for an AIDS patient, 47 percent felt that they should have the right to refuse care (with many expressing that pregnancy was the only acceptable excuse). Sixty-three percent felt that infection control precautions exercised at their facility were sufficient, while 27 percent felt that they were not. An overwhelming number (97 percent) want the diagnosis of AIDS or HIV infection disclosed to the nurse.

When asked what would be most helpful to nurses working with AIDS, 72 percent wanted factual information about risk to the care provider, and 70 percent wanted assurance of disclosure of diagnosis to the staff. Over 50 percent of the nurses wanted more information about the disease process and about their hospital's procedures regarding AIDS care. Nurses also expressed a desire for counseling services on how best to support AIDS patients (51 percent) and for opportunities to ventilate their concerns (46 percent).

G. Van Servellen, C. Lewis, and B. Leake conducted a similar survey of 1,019 registered nurses practicing in California.[7] The researchers found that while the vast majority of nurses chose appropriate infection control precautions (81.6 percent) and correctly identified high-risk group members (68.7 percent), only 11.9 percent could correctly identify AIDS versus non-AIDS symptoms. The study also determined that 91.3 percent of the nurses did not routinely take patients' sexual histories.

In determining attitudes and fears, the surveyors found that 24.5 percent still perceived a moderate to high risk of contagion in occupational/environmental exposure and 38.4 percent expressed a moderate to great degree of discomfort in caring for AIDS patients. A very high percentage (82.9 percent) expressed moderate to considerable discomfort in discussing sexual matters with homosexuals. When asked about their willingness to accept a job caring for AIDS patients, 23.1 percent indicated they would absolutely not accept a job caring for AIDS patients and 10.2 percent would accept such a job very reluctantly. As in the previous study, 53.6 percent felt that nurses should be allowed the option to refuse to care for AIDS patients.

Both of the recent surveys conducted by Brennan and Van Servellen suggest that concerns over contagion and adequacy of infection control precautions persist despite four more years (since 1984) of experience with AIDS. Certainly, reports of health-care workers who have become seropositive for HIV have caused doubts on the part of many staff about the validity and credibility of infection control policies. Nurses' fears and negative attitudes also persist, with roughly one-third of recently polled nurses expressing discomfort with or even dislike for giving care to individuals with AIDS. It is disquieting that such a great proportion of nurses do express these feelings; these findings underscore the urgency for a major effort to understand why such emotions exist and how best to resolve them. Interestingly, the surveys revealed that the nurses could identify their own need for assistance and education in how best to counsel and support the patient.

S. Geis and R. Fuller observed for one year the impact of AIDS patients on hospice staff who had direct involvement in their care.[8] The researchers found three major issues: fear of contagion, unresolved feelings about sex and sexual preference, and embarrassment over irrational responses to AIDS. Fear of contagion despite educational information, arousal of homophobic reactions, and confrontation with their own sexuality created conflict with respondents' perceptions of themselves as professional, loving caregivers. Finally, embarrassment was also expressed over irrational acts such as washing their clothes immediately after returning from an AIDS patient's home or throwing away a food gift made by a housemate of an AIDS patient.

Homophobia

F. Trieber, D. Shaw, and R. Malcolm studied the psychological impact of AIDS on health-care personnel.[9] Of the 8 nurses included in this study, all cited an increased feeling of anxiety during times of direct patient contact. AIDS patients were perceived by nursing staff to be more difficult to manage and more demanding and resistant during routine medical procedures than non-AIDS patients. These feelings and perceptions were more strongly felt by the nursing staff than by the medical staff. Caring for AIDS patients also caused more frequent rumination and worry during non-working hours, especially over the possibility of contagion of family and friends.

C. Douglas, C. Kalman, and T. Kalman looked specifically at health-care providers' attitudes about homosexuality and found that physicians and nurses in a large urban teaching hospital had scores indicating low-grade homophobia.[10] All 128 respondents had previously cared for an AIDS patient. Of the nurses surveyed, 32 percent agreed with the statement that AIDS patients received inferior care compared to other patients; 30 percent agreed that they felt more negatively about homosexuality since the emergence of AIDS; and 12 percent agreed with the statement that homosexuals who developed AIDS were getting what they deserved. The researchers found that in this group, women were more homophobic than men. Nurses who had gay friends, relatives, or gay colleagues had lower homophobia scores than those who did not. Douglas points to the ramifications for the quality of health care of such an unacceptably high percentage of professionals who acknowledge even greater negative and hostile feelings toward homosexuals as a result of the emergence of the AIDS epidemic.

More directly, J. Kelly et al. conducted a study to determine attitudes toward AIDS and patients with gay life-styles.[11] Vignettes were given to 166 nurses in which the only differences were that the patient had either AIDS or leukemia and was either homosexual or heterosexual. Study results indicated that nurses had more negative attitudes toward the patient labeled as having AIDS than toward the identically described patient with leukemia. A similar pattern of negativity was found in the vignette about the individual labeled as homosexual, regardless of whether he had AIDS or leukemia. Such attitudes included feelings that the individuals were responsible for what had happened to them, that they were deserving of what had happened to them, that they were dangerous to others, that their deaths were of less importance, and that they were deserving of quarantine. The findings also suggested that the nurses responded to the homosexual patients and the AIDS patients with nearly identical negative attitudes. The researchers suggest that nurses with such homophobic feelings will have difficulty establishing positive, non-judgmental relationships with gay patients. Conversely, a nurse's lack of empathy or concern may elicit distrust from the individual with AIDS, thus precluding the establishment of any relationship.

B. Barrick surveyed 208 registered nurses from an urban hospital in northern California to determine if there was a correlation between nurses' attitudes about homosexuality and their willingness to care for an AIDS patient.[12] The study revealed that a positive attitude toward gay men and lesbians correlated positively with the willingness to care for AIDS patients. Negative attitudes toward homosexuals correlated with unwillingness to work with AIDS patients. The survey found more anti-homosexual attitudes among women than men. It also found that 25 percent of respondents felt AIDS patients should be quarantined and that 9 percent would refuse assignment to an AIDS patient. Barrick noted that programs designed to normalize relations with homosexual patients are key to increasing the nurse's willingness to care for people with AIDS and that nurse managers and educators need to be sensitive to anti-homosexual bias as it is manifested in nursing care.

Nurses in School

In a survey of 142 graduate and baccalaureate nursing students, K. Wiley, L. Heath, and M. Acklin found that 54 percent agreed with the statement that health-care workers should be allowed to refuse to care for HIV-seropositive patients; 75 percent agreed that all patients should be required to have HIV antibody tests on admission; and 87 percent agreed that all personnel involved in the patient's care should have access to HIV antibody test results. When asked whether they would refuse to treat patients with AIDS, 36 percent stated they would refuse to provide care.[13]

D. Royse and B. Birge examined homophobia and attitudes toward AIDS patients among health-care students.[14] Of the 213 students surveyed, 68 were undergraduate and graduate nursing students. Low homophobia scores were found in 54 percent of all respondents. Greater homophobia in individual students was associated with less empathy for AIDS patients and greater fear of the disease.

A study by L. Lester and B. Beard of 177 baccalaureate students at a midwestern nursing program revealed that 96.6 percent agreed that AIDS patients were entitled to the same care as other patients.[15] However, 49 percent preferred not to care for AIDS patients, and 36.2 percent stated that they should not be assigned to them. Only 33.3 percent were willing to care for these patients. The majority of students (83–85 percent) had no prior acquaintance nor direct care experience with an AIDS patient. Seventeen percent indicated they would quit their jobs rather than care for someone with AIDS, and 62 percent felt more sympathy for non-homosexual AIDS patients.

In a survey of 242 nursing schools across the nation, V. Carwein and C. Bowles found that 86 percent of responding schools had no guidelines or policies for addressing AIDS issues, and 49 percent had no plans to develop any.[16] Most respondents felt that a student who refused assignment to an AIDS patient should be given another assignment and then counseled regarding AIDS care and transmission.

Teaching Methodologies

Is education that includes only information sufficient in allaying staff concerns? Kelly et al. suggested that nurses may need additional or better preparation to assist them in interacting non-judgmentally with individuals who differ from them and in learning more about the lifestyles and related health concerns of homosexual and bisexual minorities.[11] Attitude examination exercises are a suggested means for accomplishing this.

J. Turner and co-investigators compared a control group of 49 RNs to 149 RNs enrolled in an experimental AIDS seminar that included a structured session on attitude resolution relative to caring for AIDS patients.[17] Pre- and post-tests demonstrated that general AIDS knowledge among nurses was relatively high to begin with. Both knowledge levels and attitudes improved with education. Moreover, subjects exhibiting greater knowledge also demonstrated more positive attitudes toward AIDS-related issues. Since both the experimental and control groups improved at the same rate, the role of the attitude resolution session in changing these attitudes is unclear.

E.W. Young suggested another teaching methodology to change nursing attitudes toward homosexuality.[18] At an AIDS workshop, 14 of 22 nurses arrived with negative feelings about homosexuality, as determined by a pre-test. Of these, eight stated that they did not want to change. An open-ended questionnaire designed to elicit feelings about homosexuality was completed and collected, then distributed and read aloud anonymously. This gave the nurses the opportunity to discuss their negative and positive feelings without identifying them as their own. It was expected that allowing such discussions in a non-threatening environment would encourage thoughtful re-examination of personal values and that confronting negative feelings toward homosexuality and understanding the risk to health care that such feelings create might initiate the desire for change. While acknowledging that this was a small sample, Young noted that 8 (57 percent) of those who initially responded negatively to homosexuality expressed neutral feelings about it at the end of the session.

J. Turner, J. McLaughlin, and J. Shrum suggested a similar model of education in which fear, anger, and negative attitudes are examined by an in-depth values-clarification exercise, designed especially for nurses who work in AIDS care programs.[19] Scientific information about AIDS and HIV is also a critical program component; it should be presented along with the human context in which the scientific debate about the virus continues, in order to effectively change and shape direct care and infection control strategies.

Ethical Framework for Decision-Making

The attitudes of both practicing nurses and student nurses are clearly central to the future ability of the health-care system to continue to provide quality care. Ongoing surveys and studies reveal, however, a relatively high degree of anxiety or discomfort, homophobia, and fear of contagion among nurses in caring for AIDS patients. Such attitudes become manifested in the avoidance of the patient, attribution of negative characteristics to or devaluation of the homosexual patient, and refusal of care.

Values clarification is one mechanism with which to address change. It is a process by which we increase the likelihood that a decision we make is as positive for the individual as for the society we live in. It is a rational process in which all pieces of information bearing on a decision are given equal worth and are then sorted according to how each one is valued. The next step entails reflective thinking about and critical evaluation of each possible alternative as it is considered.[20]

With AIDS, the refusal to give care commingles two issues.[21] First is the issue of the acceptance of personal risk; second is the issue of prejudice. The acceptance of some risk, or of the possibility of harm, is considered to be a duty for members of the health-care profession. However, when the risk of providing care is too high, exceeding the conventional and obligatory risk, and cannot be reduced, that risk may be an acceptable reason for refusing to provide care. The duty to care, then, is conditioned by the risk of harm to both the professional and the patient. How great is the patient's need for care and what harm will come to the patient in its absence?[21]

Refusal to care based on risk of contagion may have legitimate grounds if the institution refuses to supply gloves, masks, or eyeshields for procedures that require protection or if the institutional staffing levels fall so far below acceptable levels that nursing care cannot be safely provided. The unsafe conditions in both instances can be reduced or brought back to conventional levels. Conversely, if the hospital provides the appropriate infection-control supplies and procedures, then the nurse may not have legitimate grounds for refusal, since the risk is conventional and obligatory and has been reduced to its lowest level.

Prejudices, unlike risks, are negative judgments based on personal opinions about the patient. They inflict harm and are never just. Prejudice is never an acceptable ground for making any decision.[21] Values clarification can be a mechanism by which such feelings are identified and understood.[22] Homophobia is not an acceptable ground for decision-making and therefore should be discussed and understood in order to minimize its negative impact on patient care. Values clarification is the basis of several of the teaching methodologies previously discussed. Studies show that it may have a positive impact on nurses' attitudes about AIDS.

Finally, to assume that homosexual bias or fear of contagion is the sole factor in attitudes about AIDS would be incorrect. Other issues that may impact on direct care include feelings of grief, the inability to work with dying patients, and feelings of powerlessness over the inability to treat a new, complex, incurable disease.[7,12]

Conclusion

Research into the area of nursing attitudes must continue in order to fully describe all of the contributing factors. Appropriate strategies for intervention have yet to be clearly defined, but research into values clarification exercises appears to hold some promise. Nurse educators must take an increasingly active role in teaching nurses about ethical decision-making and more about sexual-preference minorities, racial minorities, and substance-abusers' life-styles. Research on the attitudes about AIDS of nurse educators and nursing school faculty must also be undertaken, since these professionals greatly influence their students. Greater consideration must be given to establishing immunology, virology, infection control, and ethics as major topics in nursing school curricula and continuing education classes.

Notes

1. J. Flaskerud, "AIDS: Psychosocial Aspects," *Journal of Psychosocial Nursing* 25 (1987): 9–16.

2. R. Blendon and K. Donelan, "Discrimination Against People with AIDS: The Public's Perspective," *New England Journal of Medicine* 319 (1988): 1022–26.

3. P. Reed, T. Wise, and L. Mann, "Nurses' Attitudes Regarding Acquired Immunodeficiency Syndrome," *Nursing Forum* 21 (1984): 153–56.

4. M. Blumenfield et al., "Survey of Attitudes of Nurses Working with AIDS Patients," *General Hospital Psychiatry* 9 (1987): 58–63.

5. D.C. Wertz et al., "Knowledge and Attitudes of AIDS Health Care Providers Before and After Education Programs," *Public Health Report* 102 (1987): 248–54.

6. L. Brennan, "The Battle Against AIDS: A Report from the Nursing Front," *Nursing* 18 (1988): 60–64.

7. G. Van Servellen, C. Lewis, and B. Leake, "Nurses' Responses to the AIDS Crisis: Implications for Continuing Education Programs," *Journal of Continuing Education* 19 (1988): 9–12.

8. S. Geis and R. Fuller, "The Impact of the First Gay AIDS Patient on Hospice Staff," *The Hospice Journal* 1 (1985): 17–36.

9. F. Treiber, D. Shaw, and R. Malcolm, "Acquired Immune Deficiency Syndrome: Psychological Impact on Health Personnel," *Journal of Nervous and Mental Disease* 175 (1987): 496–99.

10. C. Douglas, C. Kalman, and T. Kalman, "Homophobia Among Physicians and Nurses: An Empirical Study," *Hospital and Community Psychiatry* 36 (1985): 1309–11.

11. J. Kelly et al., "Nurses' Attitudes Toward AIDS," *Journal of Continuing Education in Nursing* 19 (1988): 78–83.

12. B. Barrick, "The Willingness of Nursing Personnel to Care for Patients with Acquired Immune Deficiency Syndrome: A Survey Study and Recommendations," *Journal of Professional Nursing* 4 (1988): 366–72.

13. K. Wiley, L. Heath, and M. Acklin, "Care of AIDS Patients: Student Attitudes," *Nursing Outlook* (Sept./Oct. 1988): 244–45.

14. D. Royse and B. Birge, "Homophobia and Attitudes Towards AIDS Patients Among Medical, Nursing, and Paramedical Students," *Psychological Reports* 61 (1987): 867–70.

15. L. Lester and B. Beard, "Nursing Students' Attitudes Toward AIDS," *Journal of Nursing Education* 27 (1988): 399–404.

16. V. Carwein and C. Bowles, "AIDS Policy and Guidelines Development," *Nurse Educator* 13 (1988): 14–16.

17. J. Turner et al., "Nursing and AIDS: Knowledge and Attitudes," *American Association of Occupational Health Nurse Journal* 36 (1988): 274–78.

18. E.W. Young, "Nurses' Attitudes Toward Homosexuality: Analysis of Change in AIDS Workshops," *Journal of Continuing Education in Nursing* 19(1) (1988): 9–12.

19. J. Turner, J. McLaughlin, and J. Shrum, "AIDS Education: Process, Content and Strategies," *Health Values* 12 (1988): 6–12.

20. S. Steele, "AIDS: Clarifying Values to Close in on Ethical Questions," *Nursing and Health Care* (May 1986): 247–48.

21. M. Fowler, "Acquired Immunodeficiency Syndrome and Refusal to Provide Care," *Heart and Lung* 17 (1988): 213–15.

22. B. Farrell, "AIDS Patients: Values in Conflict," *Critical Care Nurse Quarterly* 10 (1987): 74–85.

6

Removing Barriers to Health Care for People with HIV-Related Disease: A Matter of Law or Ethics?

Troyen A. Brennan

As the burden of disease related to human immunodeficiency virus (HIV) grows, more health-care workers will be expected to care for people with the acquired immune deficiency syndrome (AIDS). There are signs, however, that many of these workers may refuse to care for AIDS patients because of their fear of contracting the virus. This could decrease access to care at a time when the HIV epidemic is already increasing the burden on existing institutions. Thus, the problem of health-care workers' fear regarding occupational transmission and their refusal to care for HIV-infected persons warrants close attention well before real problems with access develop.

Fears about occupational transmission have developed relatively recently. At the beginning of the epidemic, there was little discussion of the occupational transmission of HIV, probably because the risk of such transmission was thought to be nearly non-existent.[1-4] However, in the summer of 1987, the Centers for Disease Control (CDC) reported three cases of HIV infection in health-care workers who were splashed with HIV-seropositive blood; this manner of exposure was previously thought not to be a hazard.[5] Soon thereafter, other researchers demonstrated that the HIV infection rate was much higher than expected in unselected individuals admitted to emergency rooms.[6] These reports demonstrated that occupational transmission of HIV would not be limited to needlestick injuries involving AIDS patients. At the same time, the first suit by a physician against a hospital was filed in which the physician claimed that he was exposed to HIV and developed AIDS after a blood tube accident.[7,8] More suits by health-care workers have followed.[9]

These suits have heightened health-care workers' awareness of the dangers of HIV as an occupational disease, and there are signs of changes in professional attitudes. Surprisingly large numbers of surgeons support mandatory testing and refusal of surgery for HIV-seropositive individuals.[10] Very few dentists take new AIDS referrals.[11] Thus, while the risk of occupational infection is still thought to be very low,[12] physicians and other health-care workers, as well as the hospitals in which they work, may soon begin to limit care. The debate at San Francisco General Hospital provides a disturbing microcosm of our current situation. Researchers there have demonstrated that the occupational risk of contracting HIV is quite low;[13] meanwhile, the chief of orthopedic surgery has advocated a policy of physician discretion regarding elective operations on HIV-seropositive individuals.[14] A sense of disquiet is spreading, checked only by rational arguments concerning the minuscule risk of exposure if one adheres to Centers for Disease Control and Occupational Safety and Health Administration (OSHA) standards regarding safety procedures and precautions.[15]

If health-care workers' fear of occupational transmission of HIV continues to grow, there could be some restrictions on the availability of care for those stricken with HIV-related disease. To address this intolerable prospect, nurses, physicians, and ethicists have reiterated that health-care workers have an ethical duty to treat all patients, even those who pose some occupational risk of HIV transmission. I fear that this approach may go only part way in guaranteeing access to health care for patients who are HIV seropositive. In this chapter, I will recommend that society should complement professional ethical obligations to treat with regulations and laws that help defray the costs of HIV infections contracted in the workplace. To that end, I will recommend some specific legal initiatives for dealing with AIDS as an occupational disease.

Ethical Reasoning and the Duty to Treat

Before we turn to legal initiatives, it is necessary to define the scope of health-care workers' ethical obligations to treat. If those ethical obligations were absolute, there would be little need to address legal issues. Using Patrick Devlin's analogy, the outer battlements of ethical obligations would suffice to defend justice; there would be no need to reinforce the central fortifications of the law.[16] I believe that ethics goes only part way in guaranteeing access to health care and that appropriate legal fortifications will be needed to ensure that access.

Health-care workers are doctors, nurses, nursing assistants, orderlies, transport personnel, food service workers, maintenance people, and a variety of other people with jobs in health-care institutions. All may face some risk of acquiring HIV in their workplace and, thus, may not wish to care for patients with HIV-related illnesses. It is unlikely, however, that most health-care workers recognize an ethical duty to work with all patients. No one has ever defined a general theory of ethical duties engendered by employment in the health-care industry. An orderly or a phlebotomist is generally compensated for skills and performance. There is no expectation that he or she perform according to a set of particular or special ethical principles. By refusing care because of the patient's disease, the worker might lose his or her job,[17] but few would say that the worker is being unethical.

On the other hand, doctors and nurses are members of professions that have long-standing traditions of ethical behavior and well-developed ethical codes.[18] They have ethical obligations beyond their duties as citizens. One could argue that health-care professionals may have some duty to treat all patients, including those with HIV infection, even in the face of some personal risk. Indeed, some physicians have stated unequivocally that any theory of medical ethics requires that physicians provide care for AIDS patients.[19] In addition, the American Medical Association and the American College of Physicians have both asserted that physicians are ethically required to care for those with HIV-related illnesses.[20,21]

Do these assertions by some physicians and organizations of physicians necessarily mean that there is an ethical obligation for physicians to care for people with HIV-related disease? The answer is no. Individual physicians' opinions about ethical duties are helpful as a form of encouragement but carry no more intellectual force than do opinions that doctors owe no ethical duty to treat. Professional societies' ethical guidelines are at best codifications of professional consensus about ethics. They do not themselves create obligations of an ethical nature.

To understand the scope of the ethical obligation to treat all, one must understand the difference between individual ethical obligations and professional ethical obligations. The critical elements of an individual's ethical obligations are that the obligations be self-assumed and that the obligations derive reasonably from a set of rational principles. Professional ethical obligations are those ethical obligations that exist because the rational principles that give rise to them are closely related to the enterprise of the profession. Professional ethical obligations are related to individual ethical obligations in that both are self-assumed and both involve reasoning from principles to actions.

Professional ethical obligations are meant to bind the members of the profession. Of course, there is a possibility of disagreement about them within the profession. An individual professional (or anyone else, for that matter) can assert that members of a profession should recognize a certain ethical obligation. A second individual may assert that the ethical obligation does not follow rationally from principles of ethical action and thus should not be recognized. In this case, the second individual asserts that the profession will not recognize the obligation asserted by the first individual because the obligation is not reasonable. Thus, an individual assertion about professional ethical obligations does not mean there is mutual agreement about those obligations.

Indeed, there is a dynamic relationship between individual assertions about professional ethics and the reaching of an accord about professional ethical obligations. Individuals may put forth their own interpretations about professional obligations. They will try to convince other members of the profession that they are correct in their choice of principles and in their reasoning from those principles to action. Others will counter these assertions and disagree about both principles and the reasoning from those principles to action. This lively debate can and often does lead to an accord about ethical obligations.

Of course, all ethical obligations are not the subject of lively debate. The paradigm of a debate can also explain those ethical obligations upon which there is accord. For example, physicians have argued that one principle is to do no harm; they have recognized that sick patients are especially vulnerable both emotionally and physically, that the patient's sharing of intimate details of life is necessary for optimal therapy, and that, therefore, there is an ethical obligation not to engage in sexual relations with patients. Since most physicians agree with these principles and reasoning, there is professional accord about this ethical obligation.

I term those ethical obligations upon which there is professional accord or consensus, public professional ethics. The public can and does rely on these obligations. They are the product, at least in a theoretical sense, of debate and its resultant consensus around a certain principled action. Issues that still provoke lively debate are not yet public professional ethics.

There are some reasons that the scope of public professional ethics may be shrinking. We live in a pluralist, liberal society that allows and celebrates a great number of competing values. The marketplace is the dominant paradigm. The strength of such a society is the freedom of action and expression it allows. The weakness may be that there is very little agreement in modern society about fundamental principles that should guide decisions about right and wrong. Put another way, there is little, if any, sense of a common morality in our society. For these reasons, many moral philosophers have begun to focus on contextual decisions and have foregone efforts to identify absolute concepts of duty and obligation.[22,23] Liberalism, while celebrating individual choice, tends to disrupt the consensus that is critical to public professional ethics.

This is as true of medicine as it is of other professions. Physicians practice medicine in the context of the liberal state. (Throughout this essay, I will use the term liberal as did John Stuart Mill, meaning a political doctrine "associated with ideals of individual economic freedom [and] greater individual participation in government."[24]) The paradigm of the marketplace plays a constantly larger role in the practice of medicine. As the economic organization of health care has changed, so too has the role of professional values in the enterprise of health care.[25] Patients' demands for informed consent,[26] increasing malpractice litigation,[27] efforts by government and third-party payers to restrict therapeutic prerogatives,[28] growth of "for profit" medicine,[29] and the increasing role of the doctor as an employee of a hospital or health maintenance organization[30] have all led to what physicians have termed a deprofessionalization of medicine.[31] The marketplace has brought with it a sense of pluralism and liberalism.

In this context we can address the ethics of treating AIDS patients. The professional ethical obligation to treat all patients whether or not they have AIDS has yet to reach the status of public professional ethics. Several insightful commentators have attempted to identify the principles and reasoning that lead to the medical profession's obligation to treat HIV-infected patients. E. Emmanuel has noted, for example, that "the objective of the medical profession is devotion to a moral ideal—in particular healing the sick."[32] In other words, the principle that gives rise to the ethical obligation to treat all is that the enterprise of healing the sick entails treating any and all sick people. A. Zuger and S.H. Miles have framed the relationship of principle to obligation in a slightly different manner. They argue that the practice of medicine itself requires that the physician act virtuously, exemplifying such virtues as honesty, compassion, fidelity, and courage.[33] Refusing to care for HIV-seropositive patients is without virtue; physicians have an obligation to treat everyone. J.D. Arras elaborated on this principle of virtue, noting that "in refusing to treat, they [physicians] violate their own professional commitment to the end of healing."[34]

These arguments are countered by those who assert that the practice of medicine is only slightly different from other sorts of commerce and that few special ethical obligations attend the occupation.[35] They would agree with R. Sade that the relationship between doctor and patient is contractual in nature and that the doctor's rights in such a relationship are symmetric with those of the patient.[36] Such a physician can state, "I practice medicine and I find nothing in the enterprise which creates a special obligation to treat HIV-related illness." More to the point, a physician can say to a colleague, "You recognize an ethical obligation to treat; I do not. I argue that the practice of medicine itself does not create such an obligation. Just as patients are free to choose doctors, I am free to decide who to treat." This is certainly the position taken by many physicians[11,13] and some medical societies[37,38] who assert that the practice of medicine does not entail treating all HIV-seropositive patients. When coupled with a willingness to refer HIV-seropositive patients to HIV clinics, this kind of behavior is not, on face, lacking in virtue or ethics.

It is notable that the papers by Zuger and Miles, Arras, and Emmanuel all appear to recognize the problems posed by the changing structure of the practice of medicine and the pluralism this creates. They each lamented the growth of the metaphor of medicine as business. Unfortunately, we cannot easily re-create a time in which there was less pluralism in medicine.[39] Indeed, there are many reasons to prefer the changing social context of medicine and physicians' freedom to partake in and be guided by the overlapping consensus[40] that defines the liberal state. Medicine imbued with marketplace concepts and principles of liberalism does not necessarily entail a long list of public professional ethics and may prove to be quite hostile to a professional ethical obligation to treat all patients, including those with HIV-related disease.

Of course, none of what I have said minimizes the importance of arguing for an ethical obligation to treat all. Proponents of this obligation must continue their arguments and add more convincing ones.[41] If we who believe that the practice of medicine does in some way entail an ethical duty to treat all can convince our colleagues, then we will be able to say there is a public professional obligation. At this point, however, we can only say that the dynamic process is ongoing and that there is still disagreement within the profession about the ethical obligation to treat all.

From society's point of view, however, it may be imprudent to wait for the outcome of this dynamic process to ensure that enough health-care workers, particularly physicians, are available to care for those with HIV-related disease. Arguments that physicians should recognize a duty to treat may not prove totally convincing. Indeed, the majority of the profession may continue to resist recognition of the ethical duty to treat, and society cannot afford to wait. While the professional struggle goes on, society must take steps to avoid intolerable limits on care. The pluralist, liberal society relies on legal sanctions and incentives to induce appropriate behavior when voluntary actions by individual citizens are insufficient. In light of the potential inadequacy of ethical obligations for ensuring unrestricted access to care, we must formulate the legal means for ensuring access.

Legal Sanctions and Incentives

To ensure that health professionals and hospitals will treat patients with HIV-related disease, society could rely on legal sanctions such as common law actions brought by individual patients and/or on statutes or regulations adopted by governmental and administrative agencies. Fear of these sanctions would lead health-care professionals as well as hospitals to defer any limitations on care based on HIV seropositivity. Legal incentives, on the other hand, would include measures that provide benefits of some sort to health-care workers or hospitals. In the context of the fear of occupationally related HIV transmission, incentives would center on benefits that help defray the costs of accidents. For the sake of clarity, it is best to address sanctions and incentives separately and to realize that the two approaches are complementary, not mutually exclusive. Indeed, sanctions may be appropriate for certain classes of physicians, such as specialists, and for health-care institutions, whereas incentives may be more efficacious for primary care practitioners and nurses. Perhaps more importantly, legal sanctions and/or incentives apply not only to professionals but to all health-care workers and institutions, whereas ethical obligations are usually applied only to professionals.

Sanctions

The legal sanctions that can be used to regulate the relationship between individual doctors and patients are relatively ineffectual. The paradigm for establishment of the doctor-patient relationship has long been one of contract.[42] In common law, physicians have been allowed to refuse to care for patients in non-emergency settings. Physicians are also allowed to limit their practices to certain kinds of problems or to certain sub-specialties.[43] However, once a physician begins to treat a patient, a relationship is assumed and care must be continued until the patient no longer needs treatment for this specific problem.[44] This does not mean that a physician must continue to treat a patient until the patient decides to go elsewhere for therapy; the physician may end the relationship after giving the patient who is not acutely ill adequate notice so that the patient can find a new physician.[45] If a physician ends the doctor-patient relationship while the patient is in need of care, the physician may be found to be in breach of the implied contract and a patient may sue under the doctrine of abandonment.[46-48] The abandonment doctrine prohibits a physician from unilaterally refusing to care for a patient once a relationship has been initiated, unless that patient is stable and sufficient notice is given of the physician's intention to withdraw from the relationship.

The abandonment doctrine will have a relatively small role to play in assuring access to health care for patients with AIDS. If a physician were treating a patient who has AIDS, he or she could withdraw but would have to give ample warning and recommend another physician. Moreover, the physician could not withdraw if the AIDS patient were ill. AIDS patients are frequently ill, and many times the illness is critical. Does this mean that once a physician enters a relationship with an AIDS patient, he or she is committed to treatment of that patient for life? Some commentators have answered this question in the affirmative,[49] but I think this demonstrates an incomplete understanding of the clinical course of AIDS as well as the law of abandonment. The disease tends to smolder and then flare with a new opportunistic infection. There are times in the majority of AIDS patients' courses of disease in which they are quite stable, and a new therapeutic relationship could be forged without detriment to the patient. Moreover, the care of patients with AIDS is becoming more sophisticated, and primary care practitioners, for instance, may cite lack of specialized knowledge as the reason for terminating a relationship with a patient with AIDS. Thus, the doctrine of abandonment does not prohibit a physician's withdrawal from a relationship with such a patient.

The same is true for a patient who is HIV seropositive. People who carry HIV may be completely asymptomatic and may not require any acute therapy. While the patient has the potential for becoming quite sick, he or she is usually not acutely ill, and proper notice can be given with no problem. Nor will the doctrine of abandonment prevent doctors from requesting antibody screening before they initiate care for individuals. Since there may in the future be new drugs available to treat seropositive patients, a primary care physician could argue that the care of seropositive patients is increasingly complicated and requires a specialist's knowledge. In this way, the refusal to care can be couched in terms of concern for the patient. In summary, it is unlikely that the legal duty not to abandon patients will guarantee access to care for AIDS patients.

In addition to the common law sanction of abandonment suits, there are statutory controls over physicians' practices that could serve as sanctions against those who refuse to care for seropositive patients. Physicians are licensed by the state, and the state retains some control over the manner in which physicians practice. This power could be used to prohibit physicians from discriminating against patients who are seropositive. In New Jersey, for example, the state's licensing authority has stated that physicians cannot discriminate against patients with

AIDS or AIDS-related complex (ARC).[50] The state does not, however, require treatment if the physician states that he or she does not have the skill or experience to treat the disease. Thus, while state licensing authorities may be able to mandate that if a surgeon is qualified to do an open lung biopsy, he cannot refuse to do one on an HIV-seropositive individual, they will not be able to mandate that all primary care practitioners must care for HIV-seropositive individuals.

Hospitals and other health-care institutions are governed by a different set of doctrines than are individual practitioners. (Of course, many physicians are employed directly by hospitals,[51] and the doctrines that apply to institutions will apply to the physicians employed therein.) Hospitals that have emergency rooms must treat all patients who arrive in unstable condition.[52-57] Unfortunately, this right to emergency care at a hospital that offers emergency services does little to guarantee that people with AIDS will have unfettered access to health care. If an AIDS patient has a medical emergency, it is rather clear that he or she has a legal right to care in a hospital with an emergency service; but the law provides little more than emergency care. Once the acute medical problem stabilizes, the hospital and its employees are able to sever the therapeutic relationship.[58] Of course, the federal government, prompted by the phenomenon of "dumping" indigent patients in county hospitals,[59] has instituted sharp penalties for hospitals that send unstable patients to other facilities.[60] While these penalties will help ensure safe transfer, they do not guarantee access to health care at any particular institution. Indeed, it is likely that private hospitals will increasingly send indigent AIDS patients to county or public hospitals.

A more effective tool for guaranteeing care in hospitals for HIV-seropositive people is anti-discrimination law. Anti-discrimination claims can be brought under a number of statutes. For example, the community service doctrine of the Hill-Burton Act prohibits participant hospitals from discriminating.[61,62] Hospitals built with Hill-Burton funds cannot restrict access on any basis unrelated to the individual's need for care. Discrimination against those handicapped by disease is prohibited by the Rehabilitation Act of 1973.[63,64] Constitutional and federal anti-discrimination laws also prohibit discrimination at federal and public facilities.[65-67]

Access for HIV-seropositive individuals can also be created by promulgation of local ordinances and state laws prohibiting discrimination. Some states and cities have passed laws that specifically prohibit any discrimination against people with AIDS.[68] In addition, many states and municipalities have general anti-discrimination statutes with regard to handicaps. Their authorities may follow the state of Washington's lead and interpret their statutes as banning discrimination against people with AIDS in doctors' offices and hospitals.[69] The scope of such statutes and the kinds of discrimination they prohibit will have to be defined by clear statutory language as well as litigation.

Careful scrutiny of hospitals' policies under these federal, state, or local laws will ensure that such policies are not based on hysteria alone and that they bear a rational relationship to prevention of occupationally contracted HIV infection. Although this is an exceedingly complex question, discrimination is rarely unlawful if it is firmly based in a rational connection with a reasonable goal or policy. The difficulty in applying anti-discrimination law to physicians' decisions and hospitals' policies regarding treatment will be in determining what is rational.[70] Physicians and hospitals may be able to convince courts that restrictions on access to care make sense in light of the small, but not negligible, risks of infection. More importantly, primary care practitioners may be able to convince courts that the care of patients with HIV-related disease is complicated enough to require specialists. Thus, anti-discrimination law may do very little to ensure access of HIV-seropositive people to primary care and may make tertiary care only somewhat more accessible. The efficacy of anti-discrimination law will become clear if and when discrimination starts to decrease access for HIV-seropositive people and patients' rights advocates bring litigation.

If the epidemic continues to grow and the anecdotal reports of occupational spread of the disease persist, the amount of discriminatory action could mushroom, creating access problems for patients with HIV-related disease. The common law provides that doctors cannot abandon patients and that emergency room care must be available for acutely ill patients. These doctrines do little to create access to health care for seropositive individuals. Alternatively, federal, state, and local anti-discrimination laws require that hospitals create restrictive policies only if they are rationally related to an appropriate end. These legal obstacles to discrimination are potentially powerful but probably fall short of truly guaranteeing access to health care for those infected with HIV. In summary, legal sanctions in general carry us only part way toward the goal of unfettered access.

Incentives

In addition to the legal sanctions discussed above, there are incentives created by the law. Health-care workers will refuse to treat HIV-seropositive patients because they do not want to contract the virus, suffer disability, face personal economic ruin, and die. They fear both the physical as well as the economic costs of the accident. Perhaps their fear can be lessened somewhat if they are not asked to bear the economic burden of the accident. The law can and does shift the costs of an occupational accident. Thus, in exploring further the means to maintain access to health care, we should review the available mechanisms for shifting the costs of AIDS as an occupational disease.

Health workers who contract HIV in the workplace will likely be seropositive for life, will probably develop AIDS, and could be disabled for a long period before dying.[71-74] There will be tremendous costs associated with these accidents both in economic and in emotional terms.[75] Once these people die, their dependents will need financial support whether or not they, too, have been infected. The question of who will bear these costs is vitally important to guaranteeing access to health care. If those who could be infected at the hospital are expected to bear the costs of accidents, they may seek employment elsewhere; this would drive up labor costs for hospitals and create new incentives for hospitals to discriminate against seropositive individuals. If physicians believe they and their families will not be financially protected should an occupational HIV infection occur, they too will insist on testing patients or may refuse to care for those who are seropositive.

The costs of accidents have traditionally been shifted from the injured to other "deep pockets" by insurance and the tort law.[76] In the case of workplace injury, however, a no-fault administrative approach, called workers' compensation, supplants tort law in most jurisdictions.[77,78] Many health-care workers, including support staff, nurses, and doctors employed by hospitals will probably be eligible for workers' compensation benefits. Workers' compensation is generally available to all employees in a given state who suffer an injury at the workplace.[79] Although some courts have questioned whether professionals can be employees, most have decided that all salaried workers, including doctors, are eligible.[80] In addition, courts have confronted diseases very similar to HIV infection in the past and awarded compensation. The best examples are Hepatitis B virus infection and tuberculosis.[81-84]

The big problem with workers' compensation is that the benefits are not adequate, especially in occupational disease cases.[85] A further problem with death benefits, and indeed all workers' compensation benefits, is that they are tied to the amount the person is earning at the time of injury. This will affect student nurses and physicians who are members of the housestaff who could expect higher incomes after completion of training.[86]

Another problem is that there is usually no way to supplement workers' compensation benefits through other sources of compensation. Most states' laws require that such benefits be the sole source of compensation for an injured worker. In these states, anyone who is eligible for workers' compensation is prohibited by the exclusivity doctrine from suing his or her employer for a workplace injury.[87] One way that lawyers have gotten around the exclusivity doctrine is by bringing a third-party suit against the manufacturer of a product that was causally related to the accident and injury.[88] The tort award provides further compensation for the injured. This manner of gaining supplemental compensation for an injured person will not have wide application in HIV cases because most accidents involving blood or body fluids are attributable to human error and not to failure of products. Other exceptions to the exclusivity doctrine are also not likely to apply to HIV cases.[89]

Some health-care workers, especially self-employed doctors who are affiliated with a hospital but are not hospital employees, will not qualify for workers' compensation. If infected at the hospital, they could bring a tort suit directly against the health-care institution to gain compensation for the cost of the accident. These suits will be extremely difficult to win for two reasons. First, most hospitals are now enforcing the occupational safety standards regarding HIV transmission promulgated by the Centers for Disease Control.[90,91] It will be difficult to prove that a hospital that enforces the OSHA standards was negligent and thus guilty of a tort. Second, the health-care worker will have to prove that the HIV infection occurred at the workplace. This will not be easy given that many accidental needlesticks will not be readily recalled and, if they are, will not often be witnessed by others.

Those who can recall and prove a specific incident that could potentially lead to an infection will face the task of demonstrating that other potential sources of infection did not play a role.[92] This will no doubt necessitate an invasive examination of the individual's personal life and habits. Indeed, these problems with proving causation may also make it difficult for a worker to get workers' compensation benefits for occupationally transmitted HIV disease because even to qualify for workers' compensation, the worker must be able to prove that the HIV infection occurred at the workplace. Thus, neither workers' compensation nor tort litigation offers ideal means for shifting the costs of accidents from individual health-care workers to society at large.

Private insurance may therefore be the best option. HIV infection would create a need for health, disability, and life insurance. While more than 75 percent of Americans have some form of health insurance, and many have life insurance, they much less frequently have disability insurance.[93] Most health-care workers would not necessarily be covered for all the economic repercussions of an HIV infection. Hospitals could, however, broaden the coverage they offer as terms of employment and provide health, life, and disability insurance for their employees. This is a step that seems prudent for hospitals to take in the near future.

The insurance approach works as long as the benefits are at an appropriate level and such insurance is available. One would expect underwriters to develop insurance policies along these lines for hospitals as long as the occupational risk is small and the insurers' actuaries are able to assess risk. Indeed, one would hope that actuaries would be immune to irrational fears and that the insurance arrangements would be a cornerstone of a reasonable approach to the shifting of the costs of accidents. Even if insurers balk at providing disability and life insurance, state regulations could be used to force insurers to write such policies.[94,95]

In return for providing low-cost insurance for health workers, insurers may require some form of testing for the HIV antibody. They would fear, and hospitals might fear, that HIV-seropositive individuals would seek health-care employment as a result of attractive insurance policies available to workers. To qualify for an insurance plan, health-care workers might have to submit to testing. Current employees who tested positive could be removed from work that might infect patients but would suffer no loss of salary or benefits. Current employees who tested negative would qualify for insurance, as would any new employees who tested negative. Those prospective employees who tested positive would not be given jobs that have a demonstrated risk of infecting others. Those who refused to test would not be subject to discrimination but would not qualify for special insurance benefits. This kind of testing would probably be required to develop a workable insurance scheme for defraying the costs of occupational HIV infection.

If we can defray the costs of accidents suffered by individual health-care workers, we will create some incentives for them to continue to care for HIV-seropositive people. While sanctions may work well for specialists, they do little to keep primary care practitioners on the job. Shifting the costs of accidents through decent insurance policies would allow primary care physicians to remain on the job with less fear that their infection with HIV would bring financial ruin to their families. While this would be small comfort to someone stricken with occupationally related AIDS, it would create a perception that one's service is appreciated by society. This perception may be quite important in combatting other perceptions that often have no basis in rational risk calculation and that are driving physicians away from caring for HIV-seropositive patients.

Some Reasonable Steps

Many physicians do recognize an ethical obligation to treat all patients. They should make every effort to convince their colleagues of the existence of this obligation. In addition, they should be willing to promote appropriate legal sanctions and incentives to ensure access to health care for those who are HIV seropositive. What particular steps should be taken? I propose the following.

1. *Lobbying state and local authorities.* As noted above, state and local authorities can go a long way toward preventing discrimination against people with HIV-related illness by promulgating targeted anti-discrimination statutes. Physicians should lobby these authorities and help get such ordinances and regulations passed. In addition, state licensing authorities should be contacted and regulations developed that prohibit discrimination. Model licensing regulations should be written.

2. *Hospital staff actions.* Hospital staff by-laws should be written that prohibit discrimination based on diagnosis. Physicians should be ready to address their colleagues' fear but should be adamant about the impropriety of refusals to treat.

3. *Occupational health guideline enforcement.* Physicians should take the guidelines developed by the CDC and OSHA very seriously and actively participate in their enforcement. Employees and colleagues who fail to follow rules should be severely reprimanded. Prevention policies should be accorded primary attention.

4. *Attention to transfer policies.* Once it is recognized that some physicians and hospitals will not agree to care for HIV-seropositive individuals, a careful review of transfer policies should be instituted. Physicians should not be allowed to abandon patients, and any such behavior should be reported to state authorities and to the patient who has suffered. The same is true of inter-hospital transfer of acutely ill patients. Less-than-excellent care of a patient before safe transfer cannot be tolerated.

5. *Increased availability of disability and life insurance.* Physicians should use their superior political influence at both the state and hospital level to ensure that life and disability insurance are available for all health-care workers at reasonable rates. Close monitoring and clearly defined eligibility rules must be developed.

6. *Mandatory continuing medical education regarding HIV-related disease for primary care doctors.* State officials should require primary care doctors to learn about aspects of HIV infection, and thus be prepared to care for those infected. Even those primary care physicians who fail to recognize a duty to treat[96] should be prepared to provide appropriate care.

This list is not exhaustive. However, it does outline some of the legal sanctions and incentives we can employ to ensure access to care. Moreover, it is a political agenda that fits squarely into the liberal state and complements the ethical obligation to treat recognized by many physicians.

As such, it seems to me a prudent strategy for the potentially difficult times ahead in the HIV epidemic.

Notes

1. D.K. Henderson et al., "Risk of Nosocomial Infection with Human T-Cell Lymphotrophic Virus Type III/Lymphocyte Associated Virus in a Large Cohort of Intensively Exposed Health Care Workers," *Annals of Internal Medicine* 104 (1986): 644–47.

2. J.W. Jason et al., "HTLV-III/LAV Antibody and Immune Status of Household Contacts," *Journal of the American Medical Association* 255 (1986): 212–15.

3. G.H. Friedland et al., "Lack of Transmission of HTLV-II/LAV Infection to Household Contacts of Patients with AIDS or AIDS-Related Complex with Oral Candidiasis," *New England Journal of Medicine* 314 (1986): 344–49.

4. A.R. Lifson et al., "National Surveillance of AIDS in Health Care Workers," *Journal of the American Medical Association* 256 (1986): 3231–34.

5. Update, "Human Immunodeficiency Virus Infections in Health Care Workers Exposed to Blood of Infected Patients," *Morbidity and Mortality Weekly Report* 36 (1987): 285–89.

6. J.L. Baker et al., "Unsuspected Human Immunodeficiency Virus in Critically Ill Patients," *Journal of the American Medical Association* 257 (1987): 2609–11.

7. T. Barker, "Physician Sues Johns Hopkins After Contracting AIDS," *American Medical News*, June 19, 1987, p. 8.

8. T. Brennan, "AIDS as an Occupational Disease," *Annals of Internal Medicine* 107 (1987): 581–83.

9. Prego v. City of New York, Index No. 14974/88, New York Supreme Court, Kings County, October 31, 1988.

10. "AIDS in the Operating Room," *Surgical Practice News*, August 1987, pp. 5–11.

11. "AIDS Clinic Being Weighed by Chicago Dental Society," *New York Times*, July 21, 1987, p. B4.

12. J.R. Allen, "Health Care Workers and the Risk of HIV Transmission," *Hastings Center Report* 18 (1988): 2–5.

13. J. Gerberding et al., "Risk of Transmitting the Human Immunodeficiency Virus, Cytomegalovirus and Hepatitis B Virus to Health Care Workers Exposed to Patients with AIDS and AIDS-Related Conditions," *Journal of Infectious Disease* 156 (1987): 1–8.

14. "Orthopod Urges HIV Testing," *American Medical News*, December 4, 1987, p. 1.

15. B. Gerbert et al., "Why Fear Persists: Health Care Professionals and AIDS," *Journal of the American Medical Association* 260 (1988): 3481–83.

16. Patrick Devlin, *The Enforcement of Morals* (New York: Oxford University Press, 1958).

17. S. Staver, "AIDS Fight," *American Medical News*, October 23, 1987, p. 33.

18. B. Freedman, "Health Professionals, Codes and the Right to Refuse to Treat HIV Infectious Patients," *Hastings Center Report* 18 (1988): 202–12.

19. P. Volberding and M. Abrams, "Clinical Care and Research in AIDS," *Hastings Center Report* 15 (1985): 16–20.

20. Council on Ethical and Judicial Affairs, American Medical Association, "Report A: Ethical Issues Involved in the Growing AIDS Crisis" (Chicago: American Medical Association, 1987).

21. Health and Public Policy Committee, American College of Physicians, Infectious Diseases Society of America, "The Acquired Immunodeficiency Syndrome (AIDS) and Infection with the Human Immunodeficiency Virus (HIV)," *Annals of Internal Medicine* 108 (1988): 460–69.

22. Alisdayre MacIntyre, *After Virtue* (Notre Dame: Notre Dame University Press, 1981).

23. Bernard Williams, *Ethics and the Limits of Philosophy* (Cambridge, Mass.: Harvard University Press, 1985).

24. *Webster's Seventh New Collegiate Dictionary* (Springfield, Mass.: Merriam and Co., 1967), p. 486.

25. C. Havighurst, "The Changing Locus of Decision-Making in the Health Care Sector," *Journal of Health Politics, Policy and Law* 11 (1986): 697–721.

26. Jay Katz, *The Silent World of Doctors and Patients* (New Haven: Yale University Press, 1986).

27. Patricia Danzon, "The Frequency and Severity of Medical Malpractice Claims: New Evidence," *Journal of Law and Contemporary Problems* 49 (1986): 57–80.

28. Richard Brown, "Competition and Health Cost Containment: Cautions and Conjectures," *Milbank Memorial Fund Quarterly* 59 (1981): 145–178.

29. T.W. Marmor et al., "Medical Care and Procompetitive Reform," *Vanderbilt Law Review* 34 (1981): 1010–31.

30. A. Tarlov, "The Increasing Supply of Physicians, the Changing Structure of the Health Care System and the Future of the Practice of Medicine," *New England Journal of Medicine* 308 (1983): 1235–38.

31. T. McKinlay et al., "Toward the Proletarianization of Physicians," *International Journal of Health Services* 15 (1985): 161–27.

32. E. Emmanuel, "Do Physicians Have an Obligation to Treat Patients with AIDS?" *New England Journal of Medicine* 318 (1988): 1686–88.

33. A. Zuger and S.H. Miles, "Physicians, AIDS and Occupational Risk: Historical Traditions and Ethical Obligations," *Journal of the American Medical Association* 258 (1987): 1924–28.

34. J.D. Arras, "The Fragile Web of Responsibility: AIDS and the Duty to Treat," *Hastings Center Report* 18 (1988): 11–16.

35. J. Reed and P. Evans, "The Deprofessionalization of Medicine: Causes, Effects and Responses," *Journal of the American Medical Association* 258 (1987): 3279–82.

36. R. Sade, "Medical Care as a Right: A Refutation," *New England Journal of Medicine* 285 (1976): 1288–91.

37. Board of Councilors, Texas Medical Association, "Second Supplemental Report," November 20, 1987.

38. "Arizona MDs Can Refuse AIDS Patients," *American Medical News*, November 6, 1987.

39. A. MacIntyre, "How Virtues Become Vices: Values, Medicine and Social Context," in *Evaluation and Explanation in Biomedical Sciences*, ed. H. Tristram Englehardt and S. Spicker (Holland: D. Reidel, 1975).

40. J. Rawls, "The Idea of an Overlapping Consensus," *Oxford Journal of Legal Studies* 7 (1987): 1.

41. E. Pellegrino, "Ethical Obligations and AIDS," *Journal of the American Medical Association* 258 (1987): 1957–59.

42. A. McCoid, "The Care Required of Medical Practitioners," *Vanderbilt Law Review* 12 (1959): 549–67.

43. A. Southwick, *The Law of Hospital and Health Care Administration* (Ann Arbor: University of Michigan Press, 1978).

44. Hammonds v. Aetna Casualty and Sur. Co., 237 F. Supp. 96, 98–99 (N.D. Ohio 1965).

45. Payton v. Weaver, 131 *Cal. App.* 3d 38, 182 *Cal. Rptr.* 225, 229 (1982).

46. Ricks v. Budge, 91 *Utah* 307, 64 *P.2d* 208 (1937).

47. McCulpin v. Bessmer, 241 *Iowa* 727, 43 N.W.2d 121 (1950).

48. Note, "The Action of Abandonment in Medical Malpractice Litigation," *Tulane Law Review* 32 (1962): 834–50.

49. T.L. Banks, "The Right to Medical Treatment," in *AIDS and the Law*, ed. Harlan Dalton (New Haven: Yale University Press, 1986).

50. G. Annas, "Legal Risks and Responsibilities of Physicians in the AIDS Epidemic," *Hastings Center Report* 18 (1988): 26–31.

51. C. Havighurst, "The Changing Locus of Decision-Making in the Health Care Sector," *Journal of Health Politics, Policy and Law* 11 (1986): 697–721.

52. Manlove v. Wilmington General Hospital, 174 *A.2d* 135 (Del. 1961).

53. C. Dougherty, "The Right to Health Care: First Aid in the Emergency Room," *Public Law Forum* 4 (1984): 101.

54. Comment, "The Private Hospital's Role in the Dumping of the Indigent Emergency Patient," *Public Law Forum* 4 (1984): 141–63.

55. Guerrero v. Copper Queen Hospital, 112 *Ariz.* 104, 537 *P.2d* 1329 (1975).

56. Hiser v. Randolph, 126 *Ariz.* 608, 617 *P.2d* 774 (Ct. App. 1980).

57. Note, "To Treat or Not to Treat: A Hospital's Duty to Provide Emergency Care," *U.C.D. Law Review* 15 (1982): 1047–68.

58. Harper v. Baptist Med. Center, 341 *So.2d* 133 (Ala. 1976).

59. A. Schiff et al., "Transfers to Public Hospitals: A Prospective Study," *New England Journal of Medicine* 314 (1986): 552–54.

60. H. Treiger, "Preventing Patient Dumping: Sharpening the Cobra's Teeth," *NYU Law Review* 61 (1987): 1186–1206.

61. *Hospital Survey and Construction Act*, Pub. L. No. 79-725, 60 Stat. 1040 (1946) (codified as amended at 42 U.S.C. 291-2910 [1976], amending Title VI of the Public Service Act).

62. J. Blumstein, "Court Action, Agency Reaction: The Hill-Burton Act as a Case Study," *Iowa Law Review* 69 (1984): 1227–52.

63. 29 U.S.C. 794 (1985).

64. School Board v. Arline, ＿＿ *U.S.* ＿＿, 107 *S. Ct.* 1123 (1987).

65. Note, "Floyd v. Willacy: Hospital Policy Prognosis—Complications Caused by TTCA and Equal Protection," *Baylor Law Review* 39 (1987): 573–601.

66. 42 U.S.C.A. 2000d et seq.

67. K. Wing, "Title VI and Health Facilities: Forms Without Substance," *Hastings Law Journal* 30 (1978): 137–42.

68. Los Angeles, Los Angeles Code art. 5.8 45.80 (1985).

69. Washington State Human Rights Commission, "Statement of Policy: AIDS and Public Accommodation," draft, 1986.

70. W. Parmet, "AIDS and the Limits of Discrimination Law," *Law, Medicine and Health Care* 16 (1987): 61–67.

71. P. Zagury et al., "Long Term Cultures of HTLV-III Infected T-Cells: A Model of the Cytopathology of T-Cell Depletion in AIDS," *Science* 136 (1986): 850–53.

72. H.W. Jaffe et al., "AIDS in a Cohort of Homosexual Men: A Six Year Follow-Up Study," *Annals of Internal Medicine* 103 (1985): 210–14.

73. I. Grant et al., "Evidence for Early Central Nervous System Involvement in Acquired Immunodeficiency Syndrome (AIDS) and Other Human Immuno-deficiency Virus Infections," *Annals of Internal Medicine* 107 (1987): 828–37.

74. R. Castro et al., "The Acquired Immunodeficiency Syndrome: Epidemiology and Risk Factors for Transmission," *Medical Clinics of North America* 70 (1986): 635–42.

75. A. Hardy et al., "The Economic Impact of the First 10,000 Cases of AIDS in the United States," *Journal of the American Medical Association* 255 (1986): 209–12.

76. Guido Calabresi, *The Costs of Accidents* (New Haven: Yale University Press, 1970).

77. L.M. Friedman and J. Ladinsky, "Social Change and the Law of Industrial Accidents," *Columbia Law Review* 67 (1967): 50–83.

78. J. Chelius, *Workplace Safety and Health: The Role of Workers' Compensation* (Cambridge, Mass.: Harvard University Press, 1977).

79. P. Weiler, *The Law of the Workplace* (Philadelphia: American Law Institute Discussion Document, 1987).

80. Higgins v. State of Louisiana, Department of Health and Human Services, 458 *So.2d* 851 (Ct. App. 1984).

81. Middleton v. Coxsackie Correctional Facility, 38 *N.Y.2d* 130, 341 *N.E.2d*, 379 *N.Y.S.2d* 3 (1975).

82. Quellenberg v. Union Health Center, 112 *N.Y.S.2d* 211, 280 *App.Div.* 1029 (1952).

83. Barr v. Passack Valley Hospital, 155 *N.J. Super.* 504, 382 *A.2d* 1167 (1978).

84. Booker v. Duke Medical Center, 297 *N.C.* 458, 256 *S.E.2d* 189 (1979).

85. P. Barth and H.A. Hunt, *Workers' Compensation and Work-Related Illnesses and Diseases* (Hartford: Aetna Press, 1980).

86. Otten v. State, 40 *N.W.2d* 81 (S. Ct. Minn., 1945).

87. Peoples v. Chrysler, 98 *Mich. App.* 277, 296 *N.W.2d* 237 (1980).

88. R. Pierce, "Encouraging Safety: The Limits of Tort Law and Government Regulation," *Vanderbilt Law Review* 22 (1980): 1281–1311.

89. A. Larson, *Workers' Compensation for Occupational Injuries and Death* (Mineola, N.Y.: Bender Press, 1987).

90. Centers for Disease Control, "Recommendations for Preventing Possible Transmission of Infection with HTLV-III/LAV in the Workplace," *Morbidity and Mortality Weekly Report* 34 (1985): 681–83.

91. Department of Labor and Department of Health and Human Services, *Joint Advisory Notice: Protection Against Occupational Exposure to Hepatitis B Virus (HBV) and Human Immunodeficiency Virus (HIV)*, October 19, 1987.

92. S. Robinson, "Multiple Causation in Tort Law: Reflections on the DES Cases," *Virginia Law Review* 68 (1982): 713–34.

93. Kenneth Abraham, *Distributing Risk* (New York: Oxford University Press, 1986).

94. Southeastern Underwriters Association v. United States, 322 *U.S.* 533 (1944).

95. James Mintel, *Insurance Rate Litigation* (New York: Cornell University Press, 1985).

96. D.W. Northfelt, R.A. Hayward, and M.F. Shapiro, "The Acquired Immunodeficiency Syndrome Is a Primary Care Disease," *Annals of Internal Medicine* 109 (1988): 773–74.

7

Hospitals in New York City: A System Under Stress

Thomas Killip

The medical establishment in New York City has long taken pride in its institutions and health-care systems. With five medical schools of national renown, baccalaureate and diploma schools of nursing, a network of high-quality affiliated teaching hospitals offering postgraduate training of the highest caliber to young physicians from all over the country, and a large municipal health-care system of city hospitals affiliated through management contracts with four of the medical schools, hospital-based care was thought to be readily available and of high quality. During the past several years, however, a changing socioeconomic environment, the onslaught of the AIDS epidemic, and complex new behavior in the use of illicit drugs have altered this perception.

The hospital is the front line for diagnosis and treatment of acute illness, but New York City hospitals are increasingly showing signs of strain. Bed occupancy has increased dramatically in the past few years. Patterns of reimbursement also have been changing so that the overwhelming majority of hospitals in New York City, including those in the Health and Hospitals Corporation, have found themselves in a precarious financial position. In addition, some nursing schools have closed and enrollment in those remaining has declined. Severe labor shortages of nurses, physicians' assistants, and technical personnel have occurred throughout the region. Thus, increased demand for hospital care is confronting dwindling resources.

The hospital is only one component—albeit the most expensive and labor intensive—in our health-care system. The stress experienced by hospitals in metropolitan New York in the present health-care crisis reflects many problems that these institutions do not directly control. Health care in the United States lacks an emphasis on primary care and preventive medicine, universal health insurance, adequate facilities for home care and long-term care, and sufficient resources for drug treatment. AIDS and substance abuse have exposed the major deficiencies in our health-care system, especially in the inner city.

Census and Finances

The hospitals in New York City have the highest average census of any metropolitan area in the country. A survey in the first quarter of 1988 revealed that the average census in medical-surgical beds in metropolitan New York's voluntary and city hospitals was 89 percent and that six hospitals had a census in excess of 100 percent.[1] As anyone who is in the management of a large hospital (especially one with a busy emergency room) knows, when average census approaches 90 percent of capacity or above, the entire system is stressed. Flexibility to meet unexpected emergencies, such as equipment failure, personnel absences, or high volume, is sharply limited, and patient care suffers. It is simply not possible to operate a hospital with an optimum assurance of quality care for each patient when in-patient census approaches 100 percent.

Hospitals in New York State have the lowest financial operating margins in the country,[2] and New York City hospitals rank lowest of all. Low or deficit operating margins mean limited resources for capital improvement; crowded, poorly designed space; and outmoded equipment with increasing breakdowns. Low operating margins mean continuous scrutiny of personnel costs, the largest single item in any hospital budget, with great administrative reluctance to expand personnel to meet new conditions. Indeed, since the fall of 1987, there have been layoffs at several major teaching hospitals because of large projected deficits, despite high census. Our institutions are bursting at the seams but losing money.

Early in the 1980s, health planners in New York State concluded that declining length of stay and increasing use of ambulatory services would reduce the need for hospitals beds. In New York City, some 1,800 beds were closed between 1980 and 1985. In the meantime, the AIDS virus appeared and spread rapidly, and the world of drug abuse dramatically changed with the introduction of cheap, highly addictive forms of cocaine, which created a nearly insatiable demand among certain socioeconomic groups. New York City already had a large substance abuse problem; there are an estimated 250,000 addicts in the city.

New York is a city in which one can compete with the best and, with talent, perseverance, and a bit of luck, become highly successful. In addition, it is a town where the dweller can be essentially anonymous. New York has a high tolerance for different modes of social behavior.

Thus, its percentage of unmarried men at the start of the decade was second only to San Francisco's, and the total number was far higher than San Francisco's.[3] The explosive onset of the AIDS epidemic in a large population of male homosexuals and bisexuals and the subsequent transmission of the disease into the pool of drug abusers have combined to produce demands on the health-care system that could not have been foreseen a decade ago.

Bigel Institute Study

S. Altman and his associates from the Bigel Institute for Health Policy have recently reported an intensive study of health-care in the hospitals of New York City.[4] Hospital occupancy was 86 percent in New York City in 1987 but only 73 percent in Boston, the nearest large city, and 53 percent in San Francisco. Between 1986 and 1987, hospital occupancy increased 4 percent in New York City. The major change was due to an increase in hospital use by Medicaid patients; usage by Medicare and Blue Cross payers fell. Hospital usage was directly related to income, with the greatest increase coming from New York City income areas where 30 percent or more of the population were below the poverty level. Length of stay showed a similar trend, increasing sharply for patients from low-income areas.

From 1985 to 1987, patient days increased almost 15 percent in the nursery and on psychiatric services while following the declining national trend in other services, such as medicine, surgery, pediatrics, and obstetrics. In the two years between 1985 and 1987, hospital utilization by newborns markedly increased in New York City: discharges rose 4.4 percent; patient days, 15 percent; and length of stay, 10 percent. These changes reflect a sharp increase in addicted babies and those with low birthweight from high-risk pregnancies of mothers at or near the poverty level.

The Bigel study reported that, similarly, discharges rose 9 percent; patient days rose 14.5 percent; and length of stay rose 5 percent in psychiatric services in New York City between 1985 and 1987. More patients are being kept longer. For patients with a diagnosis of substance abuse, discharges rose 17 percent and patient days rose 14.4 percent. Discharges and patient days rose 45 percent and 44 percent, respectively, for patients with a diagnosis of AIDS. This analysis, of course, was carried out during the accelerating phase of the epidemic. Finally, the study revealed that in 1987 52 percent of all admissions in New York City were unscheduled, coming through the emergency room. In the municipal hospitals, the rate was a staggering 66 percent; in the voluntary hospitals, it was 46 percent.

The result of these changes is "medical gridlock." Demand for hospital beds now often exceeds capacity in New York City. The emergency rooms are beleaguered with a backlog of acutely ill patients who often wait several hours or even days for admission to a bed. As the Bigel study dramatically illustrated, this extraordinary growth in demand is largely attributable to AIDS, substance abuse, increasing need for acute psychiatric care, and a rapid rise in the number of newborns requiring prolonged intensive care. The latter two demands are a clear reflection of the impact of substance abuse on the health of the community.

The Bigel report concluded, "Had it not been for the growth in psychiatry, substance abuse, AIDS, and neonatal services, in-patient hospital use in New York City would actually have fallen roughly 5 percent between July 1985 and July 1987 as was expected by planners and regulators who oversaw the closure of 1,800 hospital beds citywide during that period." Furthermore, if these three components of demand are excluded, hospital usage in New York City follows national trends.

These data make it clear that New York City hospitals are facing a crisis of monumental proportions; increasing demand for services is largely driven by the effect of AIDS and substance abuse on the health of the community in a setting of increased poverty and medical indigency.

AIDS

The population afflicted with AIDS is growing and changing rapidly. The most recent snapshot by the Greater New York Hospital Association during the week of January 8, 1989, revealed a census of 1,740 patients with a diagnosis of AIDS in hospitals in New York City; this was a 4.1 percent increase from three months earlier.[5] Of these, 62 percent were in the voluntary and private hospitals, 34 percent in the municipal hospitals, and 4 percent in the Veterans Administration hospitals. However, the cases are not evenly distributed. A small group of voluntary and city hospitals carry the largest share of these patients.

The municipal hospitals, especially, are carrying a disproportionate load, since their total bed capacity is 8,288 compared to 27,500 for the private and voluntary institutions. Hence, on the day of census, 3.9 percent of the voluntary hospital beds and 7.1 percent of the municipal hospital beds were occupied by patients with AIDS. More meaningful is the ratio of AIDS cases to medical-surgical beds: 5.3 percent for the voluntary and private hospitals, and 14.7 percent for the city institutions. That municipal hospitals have a higher proportion of AIDS patients relative to their capacity is not surprising, since AIDS in New York City is increasingly a disease of the impoverished and the minorities, the populations traditionally served by the city system.

Epidemiologic data suggest that the attack rate for AIDS in homosexual males has peaked and is probably declining, but the incidence is rapidly escalating in the substance abuse population. To date, most instances of heterosexual transmission appear to be largely confined to partners, generally female, of drug addicts. (AIDS in patients with hemophilia represents an especially tragic problem.) Two years ago, at the Beth Israel Medical Center, 65 percent of the AIDS patients were gay or bisexual and 35 percent were ill as a result of substance abuse. Our most recent weekly census shows an exact reversal of these statistics. Not only has the number of cases in the hospital more than doubled, but now only about 35 percent are gay or bisexual; in 65 percent, the risk factor is substance abuse.

The number of patients with AIDS is projected to continue to increase rapidly in New York City.[6] Approximately 5,300 new cases were reported in 1988. By 1994, the Department of Health estimates the number of new cases will be approximately 12,700. By 1988, a total of 17,600 cases of AIDS had been recorded in this city; the number is estimated to reach 76,700 by 1994. Clearly, demand for hospital beds will continue to rise. An estimated total of 2,700 beds will be required by 1991 and at least 3,500 by 1994. This projection does not take into account the possible effect of drugs on prolongation of life and its consequent effect on bed utilization.

The change in character of the AIDS patient from generally white, middle class, and gay to afflicted members of the addict population will challenge the way our hospitals are run. When large numbers of substance abuse patients inhabit a hospital, pushers begin strolling the halls. Wheeling and dealing goes on in the corridors and stairwells. Patients are "shooting up," and the atmosphere of a devoted health-care environment is easily subverted. Contributing to this situation is the fact that treatment facilities for addiction are woefully inadequate to meet the demand. There is an urgent need for greatly expanded treatment programs.

Hospitals will have to determine how they can maintain control of their environment. How does one deal with the disruptive, abusive, and threatening patient? We have already read about shootings in emergency rooms as the social conflicts associated with substance abuse erupt. Careful thought will have to be given to resolving the conflicts that will arise between the need of the hospital to protect its patients and personnel and the mandate to offer care to the disturbed patient. Clearly, compromises that may not be pleasing to all constituents will be required. There will be conflict between the health-care workers, advocates for the patients, and, possibly, civil libertarians. Yet the hospital must maintain a healthy environment for all of its patients; it cannot permit one element of its clientele to destroy its capacity to give care to all.

Health-Care Workers

Foremost among the challenges from AIDS has been the concern of hospital personnel—nurses, physicians, and other employees—about the danger of infection. For many, the fear of contagion has been associated with a lack of knowledge and understanding. Intensive, continuing, educational efforts for employees at all levels are absolutely essential to avoid embarrassing incidents (such as food handlers refusing to bring trays to patients with AIDS) and overcome fear of infection. Continuous educational vigilance is required, since there tends to be a high turnover rate in employment among those who have the least understanding of the risks.

A recent survey of attitudes about AIDS among nurses and physicians at one institution in New York City found fear of contagion in two-thirds of the sample studied despite the following of preventive guidelines.[7] Almost half (48 percent) reported feeling angry at the homosexual population who, they felt, had only themselves to blame. Fifty-three percent of the respondents sometimes avoided performing procedures on patients. Minority respondents, including those of Asian origin, were most distrustful of what the experts were saying and were more uncomfortable in dealing with homosexuals. However, 97 percent of the respondents expressed a strong sense of obligation and commitment to care for patients throughout the illness, including stages of dying.

Clearly, health-care institutions must be aware of the attitudes and fears of all their employees, especially of those on the front lines—the nurses and the doctors. Focused discussion groups have proved helpful in uncovering common concerns and maintaining an objective, professional attitude. At Beth Israel, a counseling team led by a full-time psychiatrist is devoted exclusively to working with the nursing and medical staff.

The greatest risk of hospital-acquired infection is from accidental needlesticks or exposure to a large volume of contaminated body fluid.[8] At Beth Israel Medical Center, we have mounted an aggressive needlestick prevention program including intensive educational programs about needle etiquette. House officers view a movie on needle handling, participate in an extensive discussion of avoidance of risk by proper techniques, and undergo a pre- and post-session test. Needle disposal units have been placed in every patient care room in the hospital and a well-monitored routine of prompt replacement when near full is in effect. Physicians and staff in infection control and a full-time AIDS coordinator are responsible for organizing the educational effort. In addition, we have adopted a policy of universal blood and body fluid precautions. It has been difficult, however, to persuade all physicians involved in direct patient care to carry out this policy.

A recent sample of housestaff attitudes in New York City revealed the following: About one-quarter of the house officers would not continue to care for patients with AIDS if given a choice; about 11 percent of the house officers were resentful about having to care for patients with AIDS; and more than one-third of the residents in medicine and almost a fifth of those in pediatrics stated that their experience with AIDS made them less likely to care for such patients in the future. Most challenging of all was the report that 24 percent of the house officers surveyed stated that it was not unethical for a physician to refuse to care for a patient with AIDS.[9]

There have been suggestions that the high incidence of patients with AIDS and substance abuse has had a negative influence on recruiting the best medical students for training programs in New York City. Hard data are not available since the results of the internship match are highly confidential and the intensely competitive institutions are reluctant to share data. It is well established, however, that primary care specialties, such as medicine, pediatrics, and family medicine, have become increasingly less attractive to the top graduates of medical schools.[10] What impact the new rules limiting the number of successive hours of active duty required of housestaff will have on recruitment in New York State remains to be seen. However, the changing health-care scer 's overall impact on recruitment in New York City is worrisome, since the ability of the high-quality teaching hospitals to attract outstanding young physicians is directly related to the quality of the city's institutions. Declining attraction of primary care specialties, concern about the patient care mix, and its effect on educational balance must be overcome by a restructuring of the educational experience with a necessary emphasis on the positive aspects of training in New York City.

Summary and Conclusions

The current predicament of the hospitals in New York City is partly a study in classic epidemiology: An infectious disease—AIDS—in a favorable environment for contagion—homosexuality and, more recently, substance abuse with its ethic of needle sharing and poverty—is facing a poorly organized medical system with lack of access to primary care by the medically impoverished. While the hospitals have done much to help alleviate the situation during the past few years, long-term solutions will depend upon the attitudes of society and its leaders.[11]

Finances. Providing adequate reimbursement for the hospitals of New York City is a complex issue and cannot be settled here. However, the hospitals cannot be the political pawns of budget balancing at the state and federal levels. Every possible effort must be made to convince our elected representatives of the importance of this issue.

Shortages of Personnel. The law of supply and demand is alive and well. Salaries of health-care workers in short supply have risen significantly over the past two to three years. Whether this rise will have an impact on recruitment remains to be seen. The decline in enrollment in schools of nursing may have begun to turn around—a hopeful sign. Technologists in a variety of disciplines remain in short supply. Consolidation of educational efforts and cooperation among the major medical centers to provide suitable training in the clinical setting might well enhance the ability of the technical specialties to recruit competent students into their challenging fields. Such steps require money and imagination that may not be forthcoming.

Overcrowding and Increased Demand for Hospital Beds. It is highly unlikely that the projected increase in hospital beds required for the 1990s can be made available in time. The costs will be enormous. Creation of one or more hospitals exclusively devoted to AIDS—a disease that engulfs all body systems—as has been proposed by some, would create a new set of problems. The length of stay in New York City hospitals is excessively high by national standards. Yet a 2 percent decrease in length of stay per year throughout the system would accommodate the projected increased demand for beds. The shorter the length of stay, the fewer new beds need to be created. A successful and persistent effort to shorten length of stay is essential.

Skilled nursing beds and adequate home-care services are critically short of those needed. This lack contributes significantly to the increased length of stay in New York City hospitals because patients cannot be discharged unless they have some place to go. It is difficult to escape the conclusion that there is an urgent need for programs to develop such facilities, which would be cheaper than building new hospitals.

Substance Abuse. This scourge is eating at the fabric of our society and threatening to destroy the vitality of our city. It is intrinsically intertwined with poverty and access to adequate treatment, problems that this country of great riches has not been able to solve. People of good will differ on the best approaches. What is required is a sense of national urgency, money, and the most effective scientific, social, and political talent we can muster.

AIDS. Education, education, and yet more education is essential. We must reach all those at risk and reduce the possibility of spread. Since needle-sharing among addicts is now the major source of transmission, it is absolutely necessary to make available to this population effective treatment for addiction that is convenient and accessible. This approach cannot succeed alone; it must be coupled with a massive effort at the federal level to interdict drug usage. We are simply not yet organized at the national or local level to deal effectively with the problem. As S. Thier has stated, we need leadership that "stays the course."[11]

Our System of Medical Care. The hospitals in New York City are hostage to deficiencies in our system of medical care. Lack of universal health insurance, a large medically indigent population, little emphasis on preventive medicine or the concept of an available primary care physician, and a life of poverty for a large group of our citizens are among the shortcomings contributing to the overcrowding and increased demand for services that the hospitals are experiencing as AIDS and substance abuse change the face of the city. Clearly the time has come for constructive change.

Will the hospitals of New York City survive intact through the next decade? I am confident that they will, although the corporate structure may significantly change through consolidation or merger to improve efficiency and financial stability. More cooperation than is evident at present will be required, in my opinion, among the voluntary hospitals and between the voluntary and the city system to ensure optimal use of resources during the coming years. Since I am not optimistic that this will come about voluntarily, I suspect that the gravity of the situation will require governmental action. Perhaps we shall witness the creation of a hospital "czar" with authority to direct optimal utilization of resources for the greatest good for the greatest number in the metropolitan area.

Notes

1. Mayor's Task Force on AIDS, "Fact Book on New York City Hospitals Serving AIDS Patients," September 28, 1988.

2. *Hospital Statistics* (Chicago: American Hospital Association, 1987).

3. *County and City Data Book 1983* (Washington, D.C.: U.S. Government Printing Office, 1983), pp. 60–61, 382–83.

4. S.H. Altman, "New York City's Hospital Occupancy Crisis," Bigel Institute for Health Policy, Brandeis University, Waltham, Mass., April 1988.

5. K.E. Raske, "CEO Memo: AIDS Census Survey," Greater New York Hospital Association, February 1, 1989.

6. S.C. Joseph, "New York City Strategic Plan for AIDS," New York City Interagency Task Force on AIDS, May 1988.

7. J. Wallack, "The AIDS Anxiety in Health Care Professionals," *Hospital and Community Psychiatry* 40 (1989): 507–510.

8. E. McCray, "The Cooperative Needlestick Surveillance Group: Occupational Risk of the Acquired Immunodeficiency Syndrome Among Health Care Workers," *New England Journal of Medicine* 814 (1986): 1127–32.

9. R.N. Link et al., "Concerns of Medical and Pediatric House Officers About Acquiring AIDS from Their Patients," *American Journal of Public Health* 78(4) (1988): 455–59.

10. R.M. Wachter, "The Impact of the Acquired Immunodeficiency Syndrome on Medical Residency Training," *New England Journal of Medicine* 314 (1986): 177–79.

11. S.O. Thier, "AIDS: Issues in Developing National Policy," *Clinical Research* 37(1) (1989): 7–9.

8

The Economics of a Caring Approach

Bruce C. Vladeck

Most people with AIDS are poor. If they are not poor to begin with, they become poor as the combination of disability and discrimination removes them from the labor market and the costs of care exhaust their assets. Most reside in inner cities; ten cities account for perhaps half of all AIDS cases. By themselves, these two basic facts—poverty and inner-city residence—explain much of the socioeconomic plight of persons with AIDS.

In general, the poor with serious illnesses who live in the inner cities encounter all sorts of problems in obtaining the services they need. Ironically, poor inner-city residents actually do better in terms of access to acute medical care than to other services, and this appears to be largely the case for persons with AIDS as well. The more intensely ill one is, the more likely one is to receive help. Intensive care is easier to come by than out-patient treatment—or housing or nutrition.

As the AIDS epidemic progresses and attention rightfully begins to turn as much to providing services to those infected as to preventing further infection, questions of economics and financing come to the forefront. It is not sufficient, obviously, to define an optimal package of services for persons infected with the HIV virus; it is also necessary to ascertain how such services should be paid for. Doing so, however, requires an understanding not only of the socioeconomic context in which the epidemic is taking place but also of broader trends and circumstances. Analyzing how much services might cost is the relatively easy part. Far harder is determining where the money will come from, in this society, at this point in history.

Estimates of the cost of the AIDS epidemic are thrown around with some frequency and vary widely not only in their magnitude but also in the breadth of costs considered. For example, while it is possible to predict with increasing precision the average cost of medical services for a person with AIDS in a given community in a given year, those direct expenses pale in comparison with the loss to society of the potential economic productivity of a relatively young life ended prematurely. More indirect costs are generated by disruptions in social and economic activity caused by the fear of contagion, whether the fear is justified or, as in most cases, not. The most important costs of the epidemic are not subject to easy quantification, nor should they be; suffering and death are tragedies, not commodities.

Just in terms of direct services, it is clear that responding to the AIDS epidemic is going to cost several to many billions of dollars per year for the foreseeable future if we are going to meet even a reasonable fraction of the need for service. Those figures need to be put in some perspective, however. Five billion dollars per year, for example, which is probably comfortably on the high side as a projection of direct health-care costs even in the peak year of the epidemic, would be less than 1 percent of total national health spending in the United States in 1988, less than two months' increase in total costs. The most salient fact, of course, is that these costs will not be spread evenly throughout the United States or borne proportionately by all payers but, rather, disproportionately by the taxpayers of just a few localities. In other words, we are really not talking about an extraordinarily large amount of money in relative terms—compared, for instance, to bailing out the failed savings and loan associations or cleaning up government nuclear weapons production facilities—but rather about the distribution and allocation of responsibility.

The basic thrust of this chapter is, thus, not a series of necessarily widely speculative quantitative estimates but rather a review of some of the reasons that we as a society are generally so inadequate in providing poor people who are suffering from serious illness the wherewithal to subsist at a level of reasonable comfort while obtaining the care that is likely to benefit them. Many of the problems are in this regard generic; the problems of people with AIDS are not fundamentally different from those of families with chronically ill children, of developmentally disabled adults, or of many of the victims of occupationally induced disabilities. However, the specific characteristics of most persons with AIDS compound and reinforce these problems. Being identifiably homosexual or a user of intravenous drugs or, in many situations, simply being black implies an extra degree of difficulty. Understanding this context provides at least a basis for exploring ways to better address the problems of financing services for persons with AIDS.

Some General Considerations

Several general considerations should be adduced as background. First, it is important to understand the basic fact that being sick is expensive—expensive not just in the sense of the well-known high costs of medical care, but also in terms of the costs of day-to-day subsistence. Even apart from medical expenses and the foregone opportunities for labor market participation, serious chronic illness makes subsistence at any given level of income more difficult. One must make purchases of things that well people can provide for themselves, follow more expensive dietary and hygienic routines, and rely more on relatively costly services. Since, as will be discussed, income maintenance strategies dominate so much of our social policy toward disability, the added economic burden of illness has extremely important consequences for people who are ill.

Being sick is especially expensive for people who live alone. The extraordinary volunteer response to the AIDS epidemic has largely revolved around the provision of services—cooking, shopping, financial management, and the like—that family members, if there are any, can provide to disabled persons. For the frail elderly, the absence of family caretakers is by far the most powerful predictor of the need for institutionalization or expensive in-home services; likewise, people with AIDS are more likely to become dependent on formal services when family support is absent. The absence of family support is the critical intervening variable. Thus, one of the most dire characteristics of the AIDS epidemic is the extent to which it strikes people who live alone or who live with others at especially high risk for infection.

Second, the increasing recognition that public policy should appropriately be oriented not toward AIDS defined as a narrowly circumscribed set of clinical syndromes but rather to HIV infection as a chronic illness with a number of separate clinical manifestations complicates all the issues having to do with the financing of services. At the same time, and more importantly, it provides a more substantial basis for therapeutic optimism and interventionism. Viewing HIV infection as a long-term, chronic disease implies that financing issues will be more complicated for two reasons: One is the relatively obvious near-truism that in general we do much better at financing (as well as caring for) acute episodes than chronic illnesses; it is also the case, as will be discussed, that our public programs tend to respond far more effectively and expeditiously to problems that are clinically clear-cut than to health problems that are more amorphous or ill-defined.

A final consideration to be remembered as background is that putting the epidemic in the context of the inner city is not only giving it a socioeconomic description but indicating, at this point in our history, an additional degree of difficulty. For not only are U.S. inner cities almost by definition places in which social problems are concentrated and resources scarce, but the very prevalence of problems for which service resources are scarce may have a kind of interactive cascade effect. Not only do persons with AIDS need medical care, but they must receive it from an inner-city health-care system that, in stark contrast to the health-care system in most of the rest of the United States, is severely overstressed and functioning very close to, if not in excess of, its effective capacity. Not only do persons with AIDS need assistance with housing, but they seek it in low-income markets where the excess of demand over supply is so severe that widespread homelessness has resulted. And not only do persons with AIDS often require social services, but they must seek these services from bureaucracies already overloaded with a myriad of other social ills.

Responding to Dependency

Ever since the framers of the Social Security Act sought to abolish indoor relief with a prohibition on paying benefits to residents of public institutions, the American public policy response to dependency of all kinds has revolved around cash assistance. In the context of a culture hostile to institutionalization in all its forms, the guiding principle has been to give people cash supplemented with specific services. This is a policy that reached something of an apotheosis in the welfare reform movement of the 1960s when the role of income maintenance clerks was split off from caseworkers—and the casework function was then permitted to atrophy. In the contemporary environment, the most obvious paradigm is care of the chronically mentally ill whose monthly Supplemental Security Insurance (SSI) checks (even with a residential supplement, even when SSI coverage has not been illegally denied) hardly constitute a full constellation of services (which clients are left largely to arrange for themselves, if indeed the services exist at all).

It is hard to live in New York City or San Francisco on $450 a month, the approximate current level of SSI benefits, but the general inadequacy of SSI benefits is not the primary focus here. The fact that a nationally established basic SSI benefit does not even begin to accommodate the extra expenses associated with living in one of the two cities that probably have the highest cost of living in the United States is somewhat more relevant, although the states, of course, remain free to supplement the benefit. What is relevant here is that a benefit standard presumably derived (before erosion by inflation) from a determination of a minimum standard of income adequacy for people who are not seriously ill and who have friends and neighbors on whom they can rely for support is almost certain to be inadequate for people who are seriously ill and live alone.

This situation will get worse, of course, as more and more of the persons who comprise the population with AIDS are IV drug abusers without the employment history to make them eligible for Supplemental Security Disability Insurance (SSDI) and SSI. In most states, benefits for Home Relief/General Assistance are lower still than SSI. Indeed, while as a society we remain committed to outdoor relief, we have always also been generally reluctant to be too generous with income support, lest non-participation in the labor market become too attractive. Income maintenance may be the preferred strategy, but it is invariably tied to a grudging and parsimonious definition of income adequacy.

This is not to argue with the underlying fundamental principle that what poor people most need is more income; cash assistance must be the keystone of any strategy to assist poor people who are unable to participate in the labor market. On the other hand, it is not to promote a fantasy that some day this society will provide adequate benefit levels to cash assistance recipients. It is simply to provide a reminder that any service strategy for people with AIDS or other chronic disabilities must recognize that a large proportion of the clients lack even enough income to get by; providing specific technical and professional services without assistance with the expenses of daily living will leave clients unable to meet all their needs.

The Medicaid Trap

Almost from the inception of Medicaid, states have worked avidly to transfer as many as possible of the costs associated with care of dependent populations from traditional funding sources to Medicaid, and thus to a federal matching share of 50 percent or more. This process has especially accelerated since 1981 because Medicaid has been much better insulated from budget cutting than almost any other federal domestic program. Perhaps ironically in the context at hand, the two states that have most aggressively pioneered in these efforts are New York and California. Thus, almost all institutional services for the mentally retarded and the frail elderly, as well as a growing proportion of services for the chronically mentally ill and those for the physically disabled not covered by Medicare, have been squeezed into the health insurance box of Medicaid. For the first decade of Medicaid's history, the fastest-growing category of programmatic expenses was long-term care for the elderly; in the second decade, it was overtaken by services to the developmentally, psychiatrically, or physically disabled.

In New York State, this by-now reflexive behavior on the part of state policymakers has been carried to almost fetish-like dimensions, perhaps most notably with the invention of the clinically dubious and economically questionable creature known as the AIDS health-related facility. Like the intermediate care facility for the mentally retarded, the AIDS HRF constitutes an attempt by state officials, driven largely by budgetary considerations, to provide a service that is essentially residential and supervisory in the guise of a Medicaid-reimbursable health facility.

If nomenclature were the only issue at stake, what one called a certain class of residential facilities would hardly matter; but, in fact, defining institutions as being health facilities for purposes of Medicaid reimbursement has more important, baleful consequences. First, it all but necessitates a level of bureaucratic reporting and regulatory oversight that adds considerably to the cost of service. Second, it means that criteria for admission to the facility and, perhaps more importantly, for continuing stay must be fundamentally medical even though the service needs of the population for which the facility is created are determined in large measure by non-medical circumstances. Ironically, it may also mean that residents of the facility get less than optimal medical care. As has been the case with nursing homes, policymakers require such facilities to provide a minimal level of health-related services in order to qualify for status as Medicaid-reimbursable health facilities; but they are then reluctant to pay for very extensive services, which would be irrationally expensive. In this case, the mediocre may well drive out the good: The provision of adequate medical supervision may in practice be more difficult in facilities with limited health services than in purely residential settings into which targeted services can be brought on an as-needed basis.

More generally, Medicaid is still fundamentally a health insurance program, notwithstanding both the efforts of state officials to subvert that orientation and the very limited availability of very limited (and limiting) home- and community-based care waivers for certain categories of long-term care clients, including clients with AIDS. The effort to squeeze as many AIDS-related services as possible into the Medicaid box has, in fact, both delayed and distorted service development. For example, in New York State the primary responsibility for case management of persons with AIDS has been assigned to hospitals qualified as designated AIDS centers (because they are the easiest vehicle through which to flow Medicaid funds to support case management services) despite the fact that such hospitals may not be the best locus for case management and, more importantly, the fact that the case management capacity of designated centers in the aggregate falls far below need.

More basically, the dynamics of Medicaid eligibility are such that in order to qualify for Medicaid reimbursement and thus, in many instances, to receive services at all, persons with HIV-related illnesses must either totally impoverish themselves or have advanced already to clinically defined AIDS. As the appropriateness of aggressive, but expensive, pharmacological intervention in HIV-infected persons without CDC-defined AIDS becomes more apparent, this barrier will become more and more important.

Dependence on Medicaid also slows down service innovation, a result of the syllogism that Medicaid will only pay for Medicaid-covered services. One of the most exciting new services for persons with AIDS in New York City is the adult day-care program run by the Village Nursing Home in the building that also houses the Gay Men's Health Crisis. But development of that program was retarded for many months because at the time the program designers were developing the service, the State Department of Health was not licensing adult day-care services. The Village Nursing Home, in order to obtain Medicaid reimbursement, had to fit its program into a mental health category so it could be licensed by the state mental health agency.

It also needs to be understood, at least in the New York environment, that Medicaid is relied upon not only for the operating costs of AIDS-related services but also for capital financing, since the easiest course for public officials is to build a capital component into reimbursement rates to create a revenue stream from which capital debt can be repaid. But that is a very frail reed; potential sources of financing understandably look with some skepticism on the willingness of states to maintain sufficiently high levels of Medicaid reimbursement over time to maintain debt service coverage. That skepticism has, of course, been powerfully reinforced in recent months by Governor Cuomo's proposal to reduce Medicaid reimbursement for capital costs for health facilities of all kinds. In the aggregate, in present dollar terms it would surely be cheaper to finance the capital construction needed for AIDS-related facilities through direct governmental appropriations. Doing so, however, would, under present circumstances, preclude a federal matching share and would require elected officials to directly appropriate money for that purpose, as opposed to just letting those higher expenditures happen "uncontrollably" in terms of future Medicaid payouts.

The final aspect of the Medicaid trap is a little more subtle and difficult to describe, since it is essentially behavioral. It involves, in essence, the opportunity costs associated with the amount of time and energy talented public officials devote to figuring out new gimmicks to fit services into Medicaid-reimbursable categories. This time and energy is therefore not available for figuring out how services should really be configured or organized. Fiscal gimmicks may often have great intellectual elegance and aesthetic appeal, but they rarely solve service delivery problems.

Roadblocks

If Medicaid as a vehicle for financing comprehensive services to persons with AIDS or other manifestations of HIV infection is a kind of trap, it is one into which public officials at the state and local levels feel increasingly propelled by the absence of alternative mechanisms for obtaining federal financial support. The federal government used to play a major role in supporting a whole range of specific health-care services through direct grants to providers or to state governments acting as intermediaries; but that role has been eroded significantly in the past decade. The success of Congress in warding off Medicaid cuts proposed by the Reagan administration has obscured the very significant reduction in federal support for drug treatment, mental health services, and family planning. When the effects of inflation are factored in, states are left with substantially fewer real dollars to pay for services in increasing demand. Thus, while numbers are hard to come by, there are probably fewer people in federally subsidized drug treatment programs now than there were in 1980, notwithstanding the enormous growth in the substance abuse problem or the "war on drugs."

In the past, when confronted with a public health problem of anywhere near the magnitude of the AIDS epidemic, the nation would have taken for granted that part of the public policy response would be block-grant support from the federal government to pay for service delivery. By an unhappy coincidence of fate, however—unhappy at least from the perspective of state and local governments and of persons with AIDS and those caring for them—the HIV epidemic has coincided almost simultaneously with the Reagan revolution in U.S. social policy. In general, there is less help from the federal government for human services of all kinds. At the same time, it must be emphasized that with the single exception of the short-lived ADAPT (Association for Drug Abuse, Prevention and Treatment) program to pay for zidovudine (AZT) for persons with AIDS not eligible for Medicaid, the very significant pro-portional growth in federal spending on the AIDS epidemic since 1986 has been composed entirely of funds for research, education, and surveillance, along with the federal share of Medicaid expenses. These are worthy activities, but they do little to help people who are actively ill.

The unloading of federal responsibilities onto the states would be simply a matter of intergovernmental financial politics were it not that many social and public health problems, AIDS notably among them, have highly unequal effects in different communities. Worse, the communities most affected are often those with the fewest fiscal resources with which to replace federal funds. At the same time—as some of the architects of the Reagan revolution well understood—the political calculus of program expansion in an era of severe budget constraints makes it almost impossible to muster congressional support for responses to problems whose effects are highly concentrated in a relatively small number of localities. In short, while it is possible, as will be discussed below, to make a powerful, logical, and economic case for a much larger federal role in direct financing of services to persons with AIDS or other HIV-associated illnesses, doing so runs counter to prevailing political and governmental trends.

Missing Players

Two other factors that ought to be, in a kinder and gentler society, major considerations in the design of financing of services for persons with HIV-associated illnesses are not, under current circumstances, likely to be of very much help. The first is national housing policy. It is becoming increasingly clear in New York and other cities that the most significant unmet need for many persons with HIV-associated illnesses is a place to live. Some patients remain in hospitals past the time for which they need acute care, at some real risk to their health, because they have nowhere else to go. Many hundreds of infected people reside in city shelters for the homeless. The few models of supported housing for persons with AIDS that have come into existence, on the other hand, appear to work extremely well and are quite cost effective.

Between the Great Depression and 1981, the primary source of financing for the construction of low-income housing was the federal government. Since then, the federal government has essentially abandoned its historical commitment to the supply of low-income housing. The growing scourge of homelessness throughout the United States is at least partially a result. For the purposes at hand, however, the relevant point is that the development of housing and housing-based services for low-income persons with AIDS must be undertaken in an environment in which the development of any form of low-income housing is extremely difficult, and the number of low-income units nationally lost to fire, abandonment, or gentrification each year exceeds the number of new units created. The great expense of developing new housing—especially in inner-city areas in communities like New York City and San Francisco—makes the task extraordinarily more difficult.

Up to this point, between a one-third and one-half of all in-patient hospital services to persons with AIDS have been paid for by private insurers, and considerable attention has been given to issues such as the legality of private insurers testing applicants for HIV antibodies. As the epidemic proceeds and, especially, as more medical interventions are approved for persons with HIV infection who have not yet developed CDC-defined AIDS, it is almost certain that private insurers will continue to incur substantial costs for medical treatment.

Yet proportionately, in the relatively near future, the role of private health insurance in financing services for HIV-infected persons can only diminish. As the HIV-infected population is increasingly composed of those whose risk factors are IV drug abuse or sexual contact with drug abusers, of persons of color, and of residents of inner-city neighborhoods, the proportion of newly infected persons covered by employment-related health insurance will continue to decline. As services to those infected are progressively shifted away from in-patient hospitalization to out-patient and in-home care, the shift will also be from services for which private insurance coverage tends to be relatively comprehensive to those for which it tends to be rather narrow. Insurers will continue to make every effort they can to minimize adverse selection against them and to limit their financial liability for AIDS cases.

Moreover, in the aggregate, the size of the private insurance market is shrinking as a smaller and smaller proportion of the working population is covered through employment and as the continued spiral in health-care costs drives more and more employers (and insurers) out of the market altogether. Thus, while private insurance will continue to provide significant funds for services, its role will be sharply circumscribed and of shrinking importance.

Toward a Strategy

In the abstract, a relatively rational strategy for financing the services needed by persons with HIV-associated illnesses or disabilities might be based on federal block grants to the states, with the size of the grants tied to the number of affected persons. Within boundaries relative to appropriateness of services, accountability for funds, and preservation of audit trails, those funds could then be made available by grant or contract to many types of agencies capable of providing directly or purchasing any services that clients might need. Such funds would supplement, not supplant, other forms of income assistance or health insurance (including Medicaid) for which clients might otherwise be eligible. States and localities as well as provider agencies and local philanthropy might well be expected to match or supplement the federal block grant funds.

Such a program, funded relatively generously, might cost the federal government a few billion dollars per year at the peak of the epidemic. This is surely a great deal of money to spend on a domestic program in the current political and economic environment, but it is not an extraordinary amount compared to farm subsidies, total Medicare payments to hospitals and physicians, or a squadron of Stealth bombers.

Such a program should be funded primarily by the federal government for three reasons. First, although the effects of the epidemic are highly concentrated geographically, this is a national epidemic; every citizen is at risk. Public health is a classic public good, since viruses do not recognize the boundaries of political subdivisions. Second, the fiscal capacity of the federal government to raise money far exceeds that of the relatively small number of localities in which the epidemic has so far been concentrated. The sources of the federal government's revenues are far more powerful generators of funds than those available to most municipalities or even states. Finally, a long and hallowed tradition in U.S. public policy supports federal relief of localized disasters. No one questions the appropriateness of a federal response to support the victims of tornados, hurricanes, or floods. Clearly, the AIDS epidemic is a natural disaster of at least equivalent proportions.

Nonetheless, I do not think it will happen. In the broadest sense, the AIDS epidemic is only one of a number of socioeconomic calamities to which we as a society, at this point in our history, appear unwilling to respond politically. If we are unable to directly confront the problems of the homeless population, the epidemic of low-birthweight babies, or the parallel epidemic of drug abuse, it is hard to be optimistic about our political capacity to confront the AIDS epidemic.

Of course, some of the reasons that we have failed to adequately confront these other problems are closely analogous to the circumstances of the AIDS epidemic. The victims are disproportionately and increasingly persons of color; they tend to lack long histories of successful attachment to the labor market; and they tend to be concentrated in inner-city areas that are themselves stigmatized, that have diminishing political influence in a country with increasing suburbanization and continual political redistricting, and that rely on a diminishing number of overstressed institutions for service provision.

A wise colleague of mine told me many years ago that in the history of American politics, there were really only three issues: race, class, and, occasionally, war and peace. It is the unhappy fate of those who advocate services for HIV-infected people to be on the wrong side of two out of three.

9

HIV Infection and AIDS: Recommendations to the President-Elect

Theodore Cooper and Robin Weiss

During the next four years in this nation, the epidemic of human immunodeficiency virus (HIV) infection and its most severe manifestation, acquired immune deficiency syndrome (AIDS), will claim over 200,000 lives. The U.S. Public Health Service estimates that 1 million to 1.5 million people are currently infected with the virus. In the absence of effective therapy, the vast majority of those infected will develop AIDS and die. Although AIDS now kills fewer people than heart disease or cancer, its rank as a cause of mortality is quickly rising, and the primary sufferers of AIDS come from what is ordinarily a healthy and productive population group: young adults.

Stemming this agonizing epidemic requires presidential leadership. The epidemic poses dilemmas for both the public and the private sectors that will best be solved by forceful, coherent national policy. The obligation to formulate AIDS policy spans a variety of federal government departments and reaches beyond the Department of Health and Human Services to the departments of Justice, Education, State, Defense, Energy,

This white paper on AIDS was based on the Institute of Medicine/National Academy of Sciences (IOM/NAS) report *Confronting AIDS: Update 1988*. Drafts of the paper were reviewed and discussed by the IOM AIDS Activities Oversight Committee (Theodore Cooper, chair, the Upjohn Company; Stuart Altman, Brandeis University; David Baltimore, Whitehead Institute for Biomedical Research; Kristine Gebbie, State of Oregon Health Division; Donald Hopkins, Global 2000, Inc.; Kenneth Prewitt, The Rockefeller Foundation; Howard Temin, University of Wisconsin School of Medicine; and Paul Volberding, San Francisco General Hospital) and by the presidents and councils of the IOM and the NAS. The paper appeared in *Issues in Science and Technology* 5(3) (1989): 52.

the Veterans Administration, and other components of the Executive Branch. In addition, private organizations, foundations, volunteer groups, professional organizations, and state and local governments already have taken the initiative to create educational programs, formulate laws and regulations, and address other aspects of the epidemic. These efforts are an enormous contribution to the progress that has been made thus far against HIV infection and AIDS. Nevertheless, the absence of coherent national direction condemns many localities to begin anew when it comes to setting local policy and increases the likelihood that failed experiments will be repeated from place to place. Your Administration can furnish overarching direction for all segments of the government and the private sector. Equally important, the President can set a tone that encourages aggressive action yet resists hysteria and insensitivity to the civil rights of infected persons.

Furthermore, foreign leaders will turn to the President of the United States for assistance and wisdom in addressing their own countries' HIV problems. The World Health Organization estimates that between 5 million and 10 million persons are infected with HIV worldwide. By 1991 AIDS may double the mortality rate for young and middle-age adults in some developing countries, and perinatal transmission in these countries may reverse hard-won advances in child and infant survival.

This paper proposes that your Administration take several actions, which we believe will help slow the spread of HIV and limit its damaging effects on this nation and on other countries: (1) use the National Commission on AIDS effectively; (2) protect HIV-infected persons from discrimination; (3) develop a comprehensive plan for financing the care of those with HIV infection and AIDS; (4) initiate a forceful program for the treatment of substance abuse and the prevention of the associated spread of HIV; (5) institute aggressive and unambiguous educational programs and evaluate their effects; (6) ensure that HIV testing and other public health measures are employed only when their purposes are clear and their results productive; (7) bolster efforts in surveillance, case reporting, and the gathering of information about risk behavior; (8) ensure that biomedical research (including drug and vaccine development and regulation) continues to follow fruitful paths; and (9) recognize our special responsibility in international health efforts to control AIDS.

Use the National Commission on AIDS Effectively

The President has recently signed into law the AIDS Amendments of 1988, which establish a National Commission on Acquired Immune Deficiency Syndrome. Although the creation of a national commission is an important step, the commission's existence alone does not guarantee its effectiveness. Your Administration can maximize the commission's impact in the following ways:

- The President will appoint five members of the fifteen-member body, two of whom will be selected from the general public (the other three are the Secretary of Health and Human Services [HHS], the Administrator of Veterans' Affairs, and the Secretary of Defense). These two appointees should be senior experts of national stature in areas of particular relevance to AIDS. They should not be chosen because they hold any particular political ideology.
- The commission will submit its reports to the President and to the appropriate committees of Congress. In addition, however, the chairman should have direct access to you. The work of the commission will have the greatest possible effect on policy if it is widely perceived that its chairman has the ear of the President. The President can endow the commission with sufficient national stature and credibility for its advice to influence all participants in the struggle against AIDS.
- The commission is required to report its recommendations one and two years after its constitution. Although the reports will identify needed action, the commission will be most valuable if it is also consulted on a continuing basis as policy questions arise within the Executive Branch.

Protect HIV-Infected Persons from Discrimination

HIV transmission occurs through sexual contact, the use of contaminated needles or syringes, exposure to infected blood or blood products, transplantation of infected tissue or organs, and from mother to child either across the placenta or during delivery (and probably during breastfeeding). There is no evidence that HIV is transmitted by casual contact or by insects. Therefore, there are no grounds for discriminating against persons with HIV infection or AIDS because of fears that they pose a health risk through casual contact in schools, in the workplace, in housing, or in customary social interchanges. However, such discrimination does exist, and fear of discrimination discourages some individuals at risk for infection from cooperating with voluntary testing programs, contact notification, and other potentially effective public health measures. Public health measures crucial in controlling the HIV epidemic depend on voluntary cooperation; for that cooperation to occur, people must believe that they will be protected from discrimination.

- The President should ask Congress to enact legislation designed to prevent discrimination on the basis of HIV infection or AIDS in both the public and private sectors.

Develop a Comprehensive Plan for Financing the Care of Those with HIV Infection and AIDS

The average lifetime medical expenses per AIDS patient in the United States, from diagnosis to death, are from $65,000 to $80,000. In 1986, estimated total direct costs for AIDS were approximately $1.64 billion— $1.1 billion for personal medical care and $542 million for nonpersonal expenses; this figure represents 0.4 percent of total U.S. health expenditures for 1986. By 1991, direct costs associated with AIDS are projected to be $10.8 billion and to account for approximately 1.5 percent of national health-care expenditures. Although the proportion of total health-care expenditures devoted to AIDS will continue to be small through 1991, in certain metropolitan areas the economic burden to the health-care sector will be great. For instance, in San Francisco, AIDS patients are expected to occupy 12.4 percent of all medical-surgical hospital beds.

According to the Health Care Financing Administration, Medicaid provides health-care coverage for approximately 40 percent of all patients with AIDS. Public hospitals in states with stringent Medicaid eligibility requirements are faced with growing numbers of uninsured AIDS patients; the result is that many public hospitals are incompletely reimbursed for the care they provide. Medicare currently covers only 1 percent of AIDS patients, in part because they often do not survive the required 24-month waiting period to qualify for benefits. Private health insurance may pay for a dwindling share of AIDS patients as more poor and nonworking persons become sick and because insurers are making plans to limit their exposure to financial risk.

Solutions to financing AIDS health care can reflect the pluralism of the current health-care financing system. Elements of a comprehensive financing strategy could include enabling HIV-infected persons to secure or maintain private insurance through insurer tax incentives and government subsidy of premiums; modifying existing state Medicaid programs to make them more uniform and more efficient; shortening or eliminating the 24-month waiting period for Medicare benefits; establishing state risk pools; and establishing an AIDS federal grant program to direct funds to the states on the basis of a formula that reflects individual states' AIDS caseloads and resources.

- The Secretary of HHS should develop an AIDS federal grant program to the states to ensure that AIDS patients and those with HIV-related conditions have access to appropriate and cost-effective care. This approach would offer some immediate financial relief to those hard-hit states and medical institutions that currently bear a disproportionate burden of AIDS care.
- Another immediate need is to remove financial barriers to drug therapies. The Secretary of HHS should require that all state Medicaid programs reimburse for costly AIDS drugs once they have been approved for marketing or under the Food and Drug Administration's treatment investigational new drug mechanism.
- Piecemeal solutions to the problems of health-care financing must not sidetrack the need for a more comprehensive scheme. Your Secretary of HHS should take the lead in developing a comprehensive national plan for delivering and financing care for needy HIV-infected and AIDS patients. The following principles should guide the development of such a financing strategy: (1) coverage from the time HIV infection is discovered, (2) consideration of relief for hard-hit communities, (3) shared responsibility between public and private sectors, and (4) payment mechanisms that encourage the most cost-effective types of care.

Initiate a Forceful Program for the Treatment of Substance Abuse and the Prevention of the Associated Spread of HIV

The gross inadequacy of efforts to reduce HIV transmission among intravenous (IV) drug abusers, when considered in relation to the scope and implications of such transmission, is the most serious deficiency in current efforts to control HIV infection in the United States. IV drug abusers are the second largest group of AIDS sufferers and the most likely to transmit HIV to their heterosexual partners. Several actions are necessary.

- First, the Secretary of HHS should order a rapid, large-scale expansion of drug abuse treatment capacity to offer immediate access to all addicts who request treatment. Expansion is necessary in facilities that offer residential drug-free treatment, outpatient treatment, and methadone maintenance. Methadone maintenance, an effective therapy for some heroin addicts, does not treat cocaine addiction. Yet IV cocaine abuse is increasingly related to transmission of HIV

- Second, innovative intervention programs must be begun to reach those IV drug abusers who are not in treatment. Former IV drug abusers, functioning as community health workers, can provide individual risk-reduction counseling; in addition, trials of sterile needle exchange programs, in which sterile needles and syringes are provided to drug abusers, should be implemented and evaluated.
- Finally, long-term drug abuse prevention strategies are needed that begin with teens and pre-teens. Research and evaluation are necessary to determine which prevention methods work best.

Institute Aggressive and Unambiguous Educational Programs and Evaluate Their Effects

Educational efforts to foster and sustain behavioral change are the only practical means now available to stem the spread of HIV infection. Information about the modes of HIV transmission must be conveyed in an understandable, yet scientifically accurate form. The message of AIDS education programs must also address sexual behavior and drug abuse, matters that are regarded by some as morally unsuitable for description in public health campaigns. Unsubstantiated concern that frank, straightforward educational programs can encourage IV drug abuse or sexual relations has stymied educational efforts. Explicit information on the risks associated with unsafe sex and drug abuse and the way those risks can be minimized does not promote or encourage such activities. Its sole function is to help people avoid an illness that endangers their lives and those of their sexual partners and children and costs the nation billions of dollars.

- Government at all levels should continue to fund factual educational programs designed to foster behavioral change. This may mean supporting AIDS education efforts that contain explicit, practical, and perhaps graphic advice targeted at specific audiences about safer sexual practices and how to avoid the dangers of shared needles and syringes. This is the approach followed in the United Kingdom and in other Western European countries.
- In addition, the Secretary of HHS should see that more studies are conducted to determine the effects of various types of educational campaigns on specific populations. For example, there have been few systematic assessments of the effect of AIDS education programs or media presentations on the behavior of heterosexuals (as opposed to the impact on their beliefs or understanding about the disease). It is also essential to develop effective methods for reaching school-

age children, youth who are just becoming sexually active, and persons at risk for HIV infection within minority communities.

The urgency of the HIV epidemic warrants a multiplicity of educational efforts, including the use of paid advertising to convey all types of AIDS-prevention messages on television and in other media. A number of federal government entities, including the military, the postal service, Amtrak, and the U.S. Mint, currently spend more than $300 million yearly for advertising. Administrative restrictions from the Department of Health and Human Services have precluded the Centers for Disease Control (CDC) from paying for advertising in the past; the recently enacted AIDS Amendments of 1988 now allow the CDC to purchase advertising time.

- The Secretary of HHS should direct the CDC to purchase advertising for educational messages and should make certain that funds are supplied to do so.

Ensure that HIV Testing and Other Public Health Measures Are Employed Only When Their Purposes Are Clear and Their Results Productive

The ability to detect antibody to HIV has prompted various proposals for testing individuals and screening populations for evidence of HIV infection. However, these proposals must be assessed carefully to evaluate what they might add to interventions that are possible in the absence of testing. The President can encourage a level-headed approach to testing strategies by conveying the belief that HIV testing alone is not a panacea. Several considerations follow.

First, it is essential that the purpose of any proposed testing plan be clearly spelled out; test results should be linked to actions that achieve individual or public health objectives. For example, donated blood, tissue, organs, and semen can be tested and infected material discarded, thereby preventing transmission. This purpose is sound and has been achieved: The screening of blood for antibodies to HIV, combined with self-disqualification by potential donors at high risk for infection, has almost eliminated the transmission of HIV through blood and blood products. A common rationale for medical testing—to identify infected, asymptomatic persons so that they can be treated early—cannot be applied to HIV infection, since no therapy yet exists that prevents the progression of HIV infection to overt illness.

Another frequently cited purpose of testing, that knowledge of one's antibody status may encourage behavior change, is a hoped for but still unproven relation. In addition, it has been argued that uninfected persons can use the knowledge of others' test results to protect themselves from infection; or, in some situations (e.g., the military, jails, and other closed populations), authorities can intervene to protect uninfected persons by testing and then segregating infected persons. Extension of these strategies to the general population, however, is inappropriate and infeasible because 1 million or more people may be infected, the mean incubation period is eight to nine years, and the virus is not transmitted by casual contact. The testing of applicants for marriage licenses has also been tried, but such testing is costly, identifies very few infected individuals, and is not clear in its intent (if one of the applicants were infected, would marriage or pregnancy be prohibited?).

- At this time, the only mandatory screening appropriate for public health purposes is that of donated blood, tissue, and organs. Voluntary testing, however, will play an increasingly useful role against the spread of HIV infection. The Secretary of HHS should ensure that voluntary testing, combined with pre-test and post-test counseling, is available to all those who may be at risk for exposure to HIV. For example, serologic testing and counseling should be extended immediately to all settings in which IV drug abusers are seen or treated.

The technical aspects of HIV testing must also be considered. Although the current tests for HIV antibody are highly accurate, there will inevitably be false-positive and false-negative results (and the proportion of positive test results that are false is largest when the test is applied to populations with a low prevalence of infection).

- The federal government should give more attention to establishing standards for laboratory proficiency in HIV antibody testing, setting criteria for interpreting assays, and instituting quality assurance procedures.

Other public health measures should also be carefully considered for their potential effectiveness in controlling the spread of HIV and for their conformity with social values.

Voluntary contact notification, for instance, may be useful in preventing the spread of HIV infection. Contact notification programs allow local public health officials or physicians to inform the sexual or needle-sharing partners of HIV-infected individuals who are afraid, embarrassed, or unwilling to notify partners themselves. These programs are of greatest value when directed at those who otherwise could be unaware that they had risked infection.

Mandatory reporting of persons who test positive for HIV antibodies, on the other hand, should not be required at this time. In fact, the effect of mandatory reporting may be to discourage individuals from seeking voluntary testing, a cost that does not justify its potential benefit. For determining how many people in a population are infected, well-designed studies are more useful than random reporting of cases.

Bolster Efforts at Surveillance, Case Reporting, and the Gathering of Information About Risk Behavior

By November 1988, over 76,000 AIDS cases had been reported to the CDC. Of these, over 40,000 have died. An additional 10 to 20 percent of cases are believed to have been missed by the case surveillance system. The Public Health Service predicts that by the end of 1992, 365,000 cases of AIDS will have been diagnosed.

Estimates of the total number of persons infected with HIV are less certain. Methods used to estimate the number of currently infected persons rely on information that is itself uncertain, for example, the prevalence of infection in certain subgroups (e.g., homosexual men and IV drug abusers), the sizes of these subgroups, and the latency period between infection and the onset of AIDS.

It is essential to maintain reliable data on current AIDS cases, to refine estimates of the extent of current HIV infection, and to predict accurately future trends in the epidemic. Several actions will serve these ends:

- The Secretary of HHS should ensure that the CDC's personnel, space, and technical resources are adequate to the task of continuing epidemiological research and surveillance, including the development of mathematical models of the HIV epidemic.
- The Secretary should also see that adequate research support is provided to the social and behavioral sciences so that more can be learned about sexual behavior, about IV drug abuse patterns, and about how to influence behavioral change.

Ensure that Biomedical Research Continues to Follow Fruitful Paths

Substantial progress has been made in defining the genetic structure of HIV and understanding how the virus replicates; less well understood, however, is how HIV compromises the human immune system and causes disease. Understanding the processes and consequences of HIV infection is crucial to the development of therapies and vaccines against HIV and AIDS. This understanding, in turn, is rooted in all basic research in the areas of cellular biology, virology, immunology, and genetics. For this reason, increasing the amount of funds devoted to AIDS at the expense of all other basic biomedical research is shortsighted.

- Funding for basic research in all areas of biology should remain strong rather than be reduced in favor of AIDS-targeted research.

Current knowledge of the HIV proteins and their functions offers several potential targets for rational drug design. The search for therapeutic agents must also encompass the screening of existing compounds for potential antiviral activity. Both of these approaches to drug development require organizational cooperation among government, the pharmaceutical industry, and academic health centers.

Once a drug appears to be a candidate substance for the treatment of HIV infection or AIDS, it begins the long journey toward licensure. The U.S. drug approval process, which is regulated by the Food and Drug Administration (FDA), is the most rigorous in the world; it generally involves tests in animals and then a three- or sometimes four-phase series of clinical (human) trials for safety and efficacy. Although the process has been criticized as slow and cumbersome, it has also been credited with protecting the American public from the harmful effects of inadequately tested drugs. In response to the AIDS crisis, FDA has moved to speed up some portions of its review and has established a category of investigational new drugs (IND) called the "treatment IND," which allows manufacturers to distribute a drug for use (if the drug meets certain criteria) while it is still under investigation. Zidovudine (AZT), which was approved in September 1986 under a prototype treatment IND mechanism, received the fastest evaluation that has ever occurred within the FDA. In addition, new FDA regulations will allow the approval and marketing of certain drugs after Phase II testing.

However, the diversion of FDA personnel necessary to approve zidovudine resulted in a backlog of applications in the FDA's Division of Anti-Infective Drug Products. As the number of applications for treatment IND status grows, these personnel problems may become more severe. At present, the FDA is not a bottleneck in the availability of new drugs to treat HIV infection and AIDS. The paucity of new drugs is related more to shortcomings in the science of antiviral agents than to the drug approval process. However, as more promising new drugs are discovered or designed, the FDA, without additional resources, could become an impediment to speedy availability.

- The FDA's resources for new drug approval should be commensurate with the task. The need to borrow personnel from other parts of the agency should be relieved; the need for work space, which appears to be particularly acute, should also be addressed.

Although the FDA has responded with ingenuity to hasten the availability of new drugs against HIV, a note of caution is warranted. The treatment INDs (and certainly the widespread use of unapproved drugs obtained here or abroad) could interfere with the ability to execute conclusive clinical trials because new experimental drugs will be available to patients earlier than in the past.

- In light of these concerns, the Secretary of HHS should direct the FDA to seek an outside evaluation of the treatment IND process and other new regulations designed to hasten drug approval or availability. This evaluation should take place after enough time has elapsed to determine whether new regulations have unanticipated consequences for any new drugs.

The urgency of the AIDS situation has brought the traditional scientific method for evaluating the effectiveness of treatment—randomized controlled clinical trials—under scrutiny. Criticism of this method grows in part from the frustration, fear, and anger of people with HIV infection, who may feel a lack of urgency in the drug development process. Yet, carefully controlled trials remain the fastest, most efficient way to determine what treatments work. Conducting well-designed trials from the beginning will benefit more patients, sooner, than any other approach. Using poorly designed trials, or administering drugs without controls and without observing the course of disease, can lead to inconclusive results or incorrect conclusions. The widespread distribution of untested drugs makes it difficult to determine whether they are effective, especially if their benefits are real but small. These approaches could result in the continued prescription of useless or harmful therapies.

Although the best designed clinical trial would enroll the fewest people needed to demonstrate drug effectiveness, many persons with HIV infection want to participate in clinical trials.

- The National Institutes of Health (NIH) should provide wider access to clinical trials by broadening their geographic base; by extending trials to previously untapped populations including women, IV drug abusers, and pediatric patients; and by testing all compounds that appear to have a possibility of effectiveness.

The prevention of HIV infection by vaccination continues to pose fundamental difficulties. Experiments with candidate vaccines in animals induce antibodies that fail to block subsequent HIV infection. These experimental results tend to mirror clinical observations of natural infection in patients, in which disease progresses despite the presence of antibodies and other immune responses. The advent of a licensed vaccine against HIV remains a distant prospect. Nonetheless, innovative research continues and may produce more promising results in the future.

In the meantime, the FDA has approved human trials for two vaccine candidates. These tests, designed to assess the safety and immunogenicity of the vaccine candidates, were approved in the absence of proof of protective efficacy in animals, a generally accepted prerequisite to human vaccine trials.

- In the future, the FDA should approve human trials for HIV vaccine candidates only when (1) protection against infection has been demonstrated in a suitable animal model or (2) the vaccine candidate rests on fundamental new knowledge of the relevant human response that cannot be adequately modeled in animals.
- In addition, the NIH, CDC, and other relevant government agencies should begin now to plan for large-scale human efficacy trials of as yet undeveloped vaccines. Such trials are complex to design, and their results will be difficult to evaluate. Because the trials must enroll sufficiently large numbers of subjects at sufficiently high risk of infection, the sites for vaccine efficacy tests will most likely include African and other developing countries. A process should be agreed on for joint decision-making among the countries involved; the World Health Organization is currently developing guidelines for the conduct of these trials.

The development of model systems, in which an animal infected with HIV or a similar animal virus shows the same symptoms and exhibits the same course of disease progression found in human AIDS patients, is essential to the campaign against the disease. Yet there is currently no such model. Chimpanzees and other primates are less perfect but nevertheless useful animal models, but they are in short supply for research purposes.

- Plans for breeding, conserving, and otherwise expanding the present stock of chimpanzees should be examined. This expansion may require increased funding. In addition, the development of a mouse (or other small animal) model for AIDS is of utmost importance. A promising development in this area is the transplantation of human fetal immune system elements into immunodeficient mice. As long as efforts to develop small animal models are carried out under safe laboratory conditions, further work in this area should be strongly supported.

Existing facilities are inadequate for further advances in research against HIV: Very few laboratories are equipped to handle the virus safely.

• The director of NIH, in consultation with research scientists from within and without the institutes, should assess the need for and costs of new intramural and extramural facilities for AIDS research. This information should be forwarded to the Secretary of HHS and Congress for evaluation and subsequent action.

Federal appropriations for AIDS research have been growing steadily. At the present rate of increase, research funding will reach the goal (previously recommended by the Institute of Medicine and the National Academy of Sciences) of $1 billion annually by 1990.

• When federal research expenditures for AIDS reach this figure, an assessment of the need for further increases should be made. It is important to ensure that other federal research programs are not penalized by a long-term disproportionate growth of the AIDS budget.

Recognize Our Special Responsibility in
International Health Efforts to Control AIDS

The rationale for U.S. involvement in international AIDS activities is more broadly based than the protection of U.S. troops and tourists. AIDS can destabilize the work forces and the economies of developing countries whose advancement has been aided by U.S. dollars. AIDS can also reverse the child survival figures in countries where our help only recently has improved infant and child survival. Finally, some countries of the world offer important opportunities for collaborative AIDS research because they present varieties and prevalences of disease that do not exist in the United States.

• The United States has an additional responsibility to international health efforts to control AIDS because of our exceptional resources in public health specialists and biomedical scientists, the large number of infected persons in the United States, and our relative affluence.

U.S. activities in international work against AIDS are conducted by many federal agencies. In addition, U.S. contributions to the WHO Global Programme on AIDS (which provides support to national AIDS control and prevention programs and conducts global AIDS surveillance and research) were $1 million in 1986, $5 million in 1987, and about $15 million in 1988. Your Administration should plan now to provide a substantial increase in resources over the next few decades to be devoted to international AIDS prevention and control, reaching $50 million annually by 1990. Funds will also be needed to ensure that today's predominantly educational methods for preventing HIV transmission can be supplemented with appropriate vaccines and drugs if and when they become available.

Important as the above responses are, a further resource in the nation's efforts against AIDS is solely the provenance of the President—a resolve that the devastation caused by HIV infection will be prevented and its sufferers provided compassionate care, and an attitude that bespeaks the resolve.

10

A State Policy Perspective

Richard N. Gottfried

New York's response to AIDS has been both good and bad. The good news is that, on some fronts, New York has responded to the epidemic more quickly than many other states. It set up the AIDS Institute in 1983; it passed excellent confidentiality legislation in 1988. But there is also really terrible news. The health-care system in New York is in desperate trouble. Patients who are waiting for beds are stacked up in emergency rooms. Infant mortality figures that were horrible to begin with are increasing again in poor neighborhoods. Patients who should have been discharged from hospitals days or weeks or months ago cannot be discharged because they do not have access to nursing home beds or to home health care.

All of these problems affect our ability to provide the range of services that people with AIDS require. In addition, all of the problems of providing care for people with AIDS impact the health-care system. Many people have said that the AIDS problem is like a magnifying glass held on the health-care system. It highlights and magnifies all of the problems that were there before AIDS.

Bad as all this is, it is about to get worse unless the Legislature does something to completely turn around the budget direction in which we are headed. In 1987, the Legislature, following in federal footsteps, made some major revisions in the state's tax laws. They included a four- or five-year phased-in tax-cut package. As a consequence of the federal and state changes (and maybe as a result of the stock market), tax revenues for 1989 are estimated to be about $2 billion less than was projected in 1987 when the tax laws were enacted. In response, Governor Mario Cuomo has chosen to retain these tax changes and to insist that they represent a compact between the state and the business community. As a result, he has presented a budget that includes a range of cuts and freezes that is devastating to the health-care system. Over $200 million of the budget cuts are in the Medicaid program. Given the realities of matching funds in Medicaid, that translates into nearly $1 billion in revenue pulled out of the health-care system at a time when it desperately needs increased funding.

It is true that problems are not solved by infusions of money. But how can we encourage more nurses and lab technicians to work in the health-care system without paying them more? And how can we accomplish the other things that desperately need to be done in that system without spending more? Much of what we ought to be doing will, in the long run, save money; but in the meantime it will cost money. In the midst of this situation, the governor is proposing that about $1 billion be taken out of health care.

New York State has about 1,600 vacant hospital beds. These beds are vacant primarily because hospitals lack the money to hire staff— nurses and others—to service those beds. The Health Department's proposal for a labor cost adjustment to help meet some of these staffing needs was rejected by the governor, even before he started the program of cuts. If the governor's budget cuts go forward, the next thousand people who are lying in emergency rooms waiting for beds will have a much harder time finding them.

Clinic patients cannot be turned away when they are unable to afford the required co-pay fee of $3, but the state will then refuse to pay its $3 share. Three dollars is not much money, but when multiplied by a few thousand patients, another nurse has been lost.

Home-relief patients are those Medicaid patients who are not families with dependent children. The governor's budget makes home-relief patients no longer eligible for long-term care. So when IV drug abusers are hospitalized, whether they have AIDS or not, and the medical judgment is that they require home health care or long-term care in a nursing home after discharge, how does the hospital move those patients out if it cannot arrange the appropriate after-care?

The governor's budget will also cut, by about 25 percent, hospital reimbursement for alternate-level-of-care patients if they stay more than two weeks. The hospitals' reimbursement for the bonds they floated ten years ago to build new wings will be cut by 15 percent.

This desperate situation is not limited to hospitals, it exists throughout the health-care system. How can that system continue to function? How is it supposed to provide care for people with AIDS? How is it supposed to provide care for corporate executives who have heart attacks? The state has a commitment to taxpayers. It also has a commitment to the "Decade of the Child" and a long-standing commitment to a decent health-care system. It has a commitment to provide a hospital bed when a citizen, rich or poor, needs one. We are not keeping these commitments.

Tax rates have an impact on corporate location decisions. But newspaper headlines declaring that the health-care system is "worse than Beirut" must also have an impact on where corporations choose to locate. Not many corporations will want to locate their headquarters in a town that has that kind of reputation.

Everyone must act to reverse this situation. Every budget issue in 1989 ultimately translates back into the political reality of the threshold tax decisions. Just as they need to tell President Bush that AIDS is a health emergency, business leaders, medical leaders, and the rest of us need to tell the governor and legislators that we are in a desperate budget situation. Speeches about discipline and doing more with less are not sufficient.

There are a few other aspects of these issues to be noted. Decision-making—such as creating five-year plans—plays a crucial role. The key advantage to five-year plans is that they alert us to what is ahead, or to the parameters of what may be ahead, and to the kinds of things that need to be done.

It would have been better if the state's five-year plan and the city's five-year plan had induced Governor Cuomo to put money in the budget to pay for the first year of the plan. Instead, he took almost all the elements that were in the first draft for the first year of the five-year plan and pulled them out of the first year. At least all the clamor about that plan was useful; it forced the governor to stand up and say, commendably, that by no means was he suggesting that the budget comes close to paying for what we need to do in the area of AIDS. However, the next step is to convince him or the Legislature to do what is even more commendable: provide the money. It is important to emphasize that plans, studies, and reports of this kind play a very valuable role in expediting these decisions.

Another way to facilitate decision-making is to pull together what may be called a summit conference aimed at dealing with the problems of the hospital system. It may make sense to broaden that agenda to include some of the additional problems of the health-care system. In 1988, the governor convened a summit conference in Albany to deal with the New York City school system. In attendance were the mayor; the legislative committee chairs; the chair of the Municipal Assistance Corporation, Felix Rohatyn; and several other people. Some of 1988's legislation dealing with the city school system proves that this conference served a very useful purpose. It helped to nail down the fact that the city schools were in a crisis, and it afforded an opportunity for key people to sit down in one room and acknowledge it. It is consequently very difficult for them to avoid coming up with solutions. Today, in regard to our health-care system, many people are able to avoid responsibility by either pointing to someone else or refusing to admit that we are in the midst of several desperate crises. Pulling top leadership together serves some very useful purposes and allows a lot of issues to be discussed.

The final topic to be covered here is the relationship of AIDS to drug abuse. Drug abuse and the need for drug treatment programs were desperate issues ten years ago, twenty years ago, and thirty years ago. They did not become front-burner issues until white and middle-class kids began abusing drugs almost a generation ago. AIDS does not make them vital issues; it makes them even more vital issues. Maybe the two issues of AIDS and drug abuse will dovetail to promote some response.

It is an unspeakable outrage that New York has only about half as many drug treatment slots as needed and that someone who wants drug treatment might be told to go away. It has become more of an outrage in light of the well-understood connection between drug abuse and the transmission of AIDS. It turns into, among other things, a budget issue. It also turns into a "not in my backyard" issue. What do we need to do to hasten the establishment of drug treatment facilities as well as AIDS treatment facilities?

An extremely controversial part of the AIDS issue is the allocation of needles to drug abusers. In thirty-nine states in this country, addicts who want clean needles can get them for about 20¢ each. I do not know how many addicts actually take advantage of the availability of clean needles, but at least they are available. New York is one of eleven states that has taken a different approach and requires a prescription for a hypodermic. As a result, hypodermics on the black market cost about $5, and are therefore shared or rented by addicts. The paradox is that it is not a crime to show an addict how to clean his or her works, but it is a crime to make clean works available.

Needle-exchange programs are important and should be defended and encouraged. I would go even further, and I have already introduced a bill to bring New York's law on the sale and possession of hypodermics in line with that of the thirty-nine other states.

Some years down the road, when the number of people who have died because of needle-based AIDS transmission is in the tens of thousands (or more), many of us will be asked where we were when these decisions were being made.

11

AIDS: A Long View

Lewis Thomas

Something has gone terribly wrong with the way we think about AIDS and monstrously wrong with the way information about this disease is conveyed to the public. Listening to Sunday morning TV talk shows or reading newspaper stories, one might come to believe that AIDS is somehow a political problem, to be solved by the outcome of furious debates between moralists on the extreme right and their counterparts on the left. Conservative columnist and publicist Pat Buchanan and others instruct the world that AIDS is essentially a small, limited problem, politically exaggerated by the liberals or by researchers looking for grants. It is made to seem an exclusively moral matter, easily solved by correcting the unnatural behavior of a relative handful of our citizens who make up the gay community (which is already, it is claimed, well on the way to mending its ways through self-education and discipline) and the intravenous drug abusers—groups that may eventually self-destruct through intransigence (all the better for the rest of us) and that have done nothing to deserve our concern or compassion. At another extreme, not necessarily left nor liberal, but political nonetheless, are the groups whose sole concern is with AIDS as a human rights issue.

Because of the political influence of all of these people, we have obtained only marginal insights into the future depth and scope of the disease. The numbers are there, but they can only be guessed at. One might think, given the solid foundation of useful experience in professional public health practice gained in combating cholera, tuberculosis, and syphilis, that we would, by this time, have learned a substantial amount about the epidemiology of this singularly contagious venereal disease; but we really know very little. Indeed, some people in authority are unwilling even to concede that AIDS is, in plain fact, a venereal disease. We are only now beginning to acquire the numbers, by utilizing what is still a relatively small and inadequate testing program; and the numbers are still so limited that their significance can be argued either way. Some claim the data indicate that we are at the threshold of a pandemic threatening all of society; others claim the figures show that AIDS is a small-scale matter, nicely confined to the sinners among us.

Even today, there appears to be a public consensus that AIDS is something to worry about in only two limited communities, homosexuals and drug addicts, with a brief nod toward the occasional hemophiliacs or recipients of blood transfusions who contract AIDS or, in recent months, to mates of heroin users and their babies, all out of sight somewhere in our benighted ghettos. The epidemic is dying out along with the afflicted, says Pat Buchanan; be patient and it and they will fade away.

But the really urgent matter is only occasionally touched on in the press and I have yet to hear it discussed on television: Africa is providing the plainest evidence that we are, in our part of the world, only in the first stage of what will perhaps become, in the years just ahead, the most devastating and lethal pandemic in the memory of mankind. We simply cannot explain away millions of HIV infections across the middle of Africa, coast to coast, afflicting all classes, sexes, and ages by arguing that the Africans are in special circumstances or possess different sexual habits and inclinations or have so many other infections or nutritional problems that they are a special case, totally unlike our Western, industrialized selves. Of all priorities for research at the present moment, I would set the need for large-scale epidemiological and virological studies in Africa at the top of any list, regardless of cost. The epidemic is a strange, even mysterious phenomenon that needs as deep and detailed a scientific inquiry as the world can provide. I can see no reason to believe that what Africa is going through now will not, sooner or later, spread, however slowly, decade by decade, through North America, Europe, Asia, and South America. My personal view, based on hunch, is that the principal difference between Africa and the United States is that the HIV virus had the head start of a decade or more to establish itself in African populations—upper, middle, and lower classes—all at the same time.

Recent news from the Soviet Union should have shaken us more than it has. The HIV virus was spread with ease and alacrity by unclean needles through a ward of twenty-seven infants and then spread from the nursing infants to six of their previously uninfected mothers. This was not just a sad story deserving a half-page of human interest journalism. It was, or should have been, a terrifying warning. The transmission of AIDS may turn out to be much more complex and, at the same time, more easily accomplished than we have all been thinking.

We should, of course, be doing our best to educate our own populations in order to prevent the slow spread of the disease; but I am skeptical of expecting much change in human behavior, especially in the sexual behavior of young people. I have specific doubts about the effect of education, however well meant, on the problem now confronting the largely heterosexual, non-mainlining populations in Africa. Public education did not slow the spread of syphilis in Europe; for five centuries, beginning in the fifteenth, it ravaged the continent. It took the discovery of penicillin to make a difference. I lay all my hopes for the long-term future on science.

The world is in urgent need of at least two pieces of new technology that are still well beyond reach: first, a new sort of pharmacology to block the entry and spread of the HIV virus (and a likely congeries of close relatives of this retrovirus, which we will probably be encountering before long); and second, a new vaccine or a new kind of immunotherapy that will stop the virus in its tracks. We are nowhere near either achievement, but both are achievable, given enough time and enough world-class basic research. The problem, the very center of the problem, is that there is still no consensus, no real apprehension in the public mind, not even enough anxiety yet within the mind of the scientific community itself.

Perhaps we should stop calling the enterprise basic science. It is (and must be) basic research, requiring as high a level of imagination and pure guesswork as any effort in the history of biomedical science. If the word "basic" suggests that the research is not urgent, perhaps we should call it something else, such as applied research, or development, or engineering. Or maybe we should give it a totally new code-name, similar to the Manhattan Project. The fight against AIDS needs to be a defense program of that order of magnitude, and it is long past time to be getting on with it. Soon, I am afraid, we will be running out of time.

Summation: Better Care
for AIDS Patients

David E. Rogers

The Cornell University Medical College Fifth Conference on Health Policy was a powerful and sobering learning experience for all participants. To my knowledge, it was the first time that a diversely trained group, knowledgeable about problems of HIV infections, spent two intensive days looking at how feelings, fears, social attitudes, religious values, and political realities have affected our ability to deal with AIDS—the dreadful, relentlessly advancing, fatal disease that will be controlled only by this nation's best and most sophisticated efforts. What did we learn during these two days? Let me summarize briefly.

First, we learned that throughout history society has usually sought and readily found scapegoats when faced with the specter of a life-threatening epidemic. In the 1300s Jews received the brunt of the blame for bubonic plague, and many were burned at the stake to assuage anger and public terror. In the U.S. cholera epidemic of the 1830s it was our new Irish immigrants who were stigmatized and persecuted. In the poliomyelitis epidemic of 1916, the Italians, then our most recent immigrant group, were viewed as the culprits. The fact that in the early 1980s HIV infection emerged first in two groups with life-styles considered distasteful if not completely immoral by the larger society has clearly and profoundly affected our response to this epidemic. Only slightly below the surface, many Americans believe that those with AIDS have brought it upon themselves and that they are being properly penalized for their sins.

Second, and disquieting, was the evidence that despite nine years of experience with the disease and the enormous amount of factual information that has become available, public attitudes toward those with AIDS remain startlingly negative. Discrimination in the workplace; loss of civil liberties, jobs, health insurance, housing, and family support; and the ostracism of HIV-positive children have not only occurred but continue to occur. Clearly, more knowledge does not lead to swift changes in attitudes or prejudices. Our social and cultural reflexes shift very slowly.

Third, to our sorrow, but perhaps coming as no surprise, was the evidence that health professionals—doctors and nurses—are not that different from the rest of the public. Hostile and negative attitudes toward homosexuals and IV drug abusers are held by significant numbers of doctors and nurses. A surprising number believe that health professionals should not have to care for patients with HIV infection—an attitude that would have been unthinkable twenty years ago. These attitudes, coupled with some real fears about transmission of the infection, particularly to those health professionals carrying out invasive procedures, have clearly interfered with the quality of care provided to some patients stricken with HIV-associated illnesses.

Fourth, many hospitals—particularly those in the five urban areas hardest hit by the epidemic—are overfilled, overstressed, and have, in the words of Thomas Killip, "become hostages to the deficiencies in our system of medical care." AIDS has put a spotlight on our national failure to develop the long-term care facilities, residential units, and out-of-hospital programs to care for patients with long-term chronic disease; and it has magnified these deficiencies both quantitatively and qualitatively. This is most evident in New York City where the overcrowding and underfunding of hospitals, the absence of enough trained health professionals, and the lack of alternatives to hospital care are approaching crisis proportions.

Fifth, despite the national nature of the emergency, the negative attitudes documented by the conferees have not only permitted a slow and reluctant federal response, but have allowed a continuing absence of political leadership to be tolerated without a major outcry at all levels—most particularly at the federal level. It was generally agreed that virtually any other illness that involved 1 to 1.5 million U.S. citizens and threatened them with a miserable, lingering death would have evoked a massive federal response. However, the negative feelings toward the groups involved, coupled with the highly local geographic nature of the illness (70 percent of disease in five urban areas), have left many legislators not only unsympathetic to, but even unaware of, the severity of the plight of those cities. A national response has not been forthcoming.

What has been the result of these various forces? New York City, as the epicenter of the epidemic, stands out as a troubling example of how our national reluctance, inability, or unwillingness to respond aggressively and effectively to the advancing epidemic has begun to undermine a once-proud system of health care and the people it was designed to serve. Overcrowded hospitals, overworked health personnel in short supply, a virtual absence of long-term care facilities or residential units to care for people sick with HIV-associated illnesses, the serious lack of housing for and increasing homelessness among patients with AIDS, and the lack of adequate financing to support many of the most obvious solutions to the problem portray a system drifting and close to collapse. That the disease is swiftly and increasingly spreading among groups hard to reach and help even under less extreme circumstances—IV drug users in poor, black, and Hispanic communities—adds to the tragedy. The specter of potential racial and social conflict looms ahead as the city encounters increasing difficulties in admitting those with other life-threatening illnesses to our overcrowded hospitals.

What can we do? A number of thoughtful suggestions have emerged. While no crisp recommendations were formulated, there was a general consensus that certain approaches seemed worthy of immediate and aggressive pursuit.

1. *We should educate.* It was abundantly evident that AIDS education must be specifically tailored to different groups. But it was also apparent that when fundamental behavioral change is required, we cannot be overly simplistic or expect too much from education. Simply transmitting information regarding AIDS and its mechanisms of spread does little to change attitudes or behavior. Non-targeted and fear-evoking education have proven ineffective in producing material behavior change. The evidence that you can bring the horse to water but you cannot make him drink was depressing. The surgeon general's brochure "Understanding AIDS" was sent to every U.S. household. That only 19 percent of those who received it actually read any part of it carefully was not encouraging. That 72 percent of nurses or nursing students, even after careful education regarding AIDS, continue to believe that AIDS can be transmitted by shared coffee cups was devastating. Abundantly evident was the paucity of knowledge about the educational inputs actually needed to create behavioral change. The identification and encouragement of those working in this area deserve immediate and strong support.

2. *We should set tough institutional behavioral norms.* While it was overwhelmingly apparent that we cannot swiftly change individuals' hostile or negative attitudes and feelings about homosexuality, IV drug abuse, or certain kinds of patients, it was recognized that clear and uncompromising institutional leadership, behavior, and norms outlawing negative or hostile behavior toward any patient by any hospital staff member could facilitate profound behavioral differences. Institutions that expected and reinforced high standards of behavior toward others clearly

had much better track records for compassionate caring than those that failed to set such standards.

3. *Identifying those who wish to work with HIV-infected patients should be encouraged.* Although there was less agreement on this point, evidence presented suggested that those AIDS units in which volunteers had been recruited to work with HIV patients had a much better track record of administering compassionate care than those that did not. The main disagreement was a general unwillingness to permit some health professionals to opt out of caring for AIDS patients simply because of their own negative attitudes. At the same time, it was agreed that those who wished to work with such patients performed better.

4. *Efforts should be made to change the faceless image of the AIDS patient.* The group agreed that society has created blank-faced stereotypes of gay males and IV drug users that interfere with people's perceptions of the specific, individual suffering that accompanies the illness.

The myths that have homogenized the gay male or the IV drug user need to be dispelled so that all infected patients receive compassionate, personalized attention.

5. *We should develop adequate care services.* Clearly, new services are needed at all levels. Many must be flexible, humane, out-of-hospital programs. Decompressing the hospitals, developing AIDS units, and fostering a climate that permits health professionals—physicians, nurses, social workers, and others—to work cooperatively to take better care of patients with this complex disease will help to change attitudes. The increasing evidence that good health care can change the outlook and improve the lot of HIV patients is beginning to alter the attitudes of health professionals toward these patients. A feeling of usefulness and effectiveness much improves health professionals' performance.

6. *We should legislate.* Troyen Brennan's chapter brought home forcibly the point that good will and good intentions are not enough. We need tough, unequivocal legislation with swift sanctions for breaches in confidentiality or discrimination against HIV-positive individuals and patients with AIDS. This requires use of and recourse to the legal system.

7. *We should pay the bills required to conquer HIV infection.* As eloquently pointed out by Bruce Vladeck, this is not the best of times to get new or additional financing for research or services that would move us toward the kindlier, friendlier future we all seek. He pointed out that, grotesquely, terminal care in an intensive care unit is vastly easier to finance than simple housing or adequate nutrition. Further, he noted that the groups now increasingly affected by AIDS have less of everything: less money, less education, less housing, fewer jobs, less food, and less social acceptance. There was no disagreement on the point that we must launch a broadly funded attack on AIDS. While the costs are significant,

they are trivial when compared with the funds we spend on heart disease or cancer, or those that will be required to bail out our savings and loan associations, or to clean up our nuclear weapons waste. It was pointed out that in 1988 we spent less than 1/400 of 1 percent of our health-care budget on AIDS and that even if we reach the generous level of spending of $5 billion nationally per year, we would be spending less than 1 percent of our 1989 health-care dollars on AIDS.

Changing attitudes and behavior could improve our response to the epidemic of our times. But the problem remains—how do we secure the new funding that is needed? General agreement emerged that those concerned with AIDS must build broader coalitions to get the job done. Mere appeals for help for those who have AIDS will not be sufficient. A broadened coalition must include the support of the corporate world, the powerful presence of health professionals who clearly and unequivocally point out the enormous hazards AIDS poses to our entire system of health care, and a clearer public understanding that what has happened in Africa, where AIDS is now a widespread heterosexual disease, will inevitably happen in the United States. The public must realize that the health-care industry—now the third largest employer in the United States and an enormous source of jobs and income—is reeling, particularly in some of our major cities, because of AIDS and that it must protect and support this sector of our society and economy. To develop such a coalition the appeal must be simple, and it should push for federal assistance in areas where it is not yet involved.

These are the major suggestions for change that emerged. But there was one additional point of agreement: By a personal demonstration of tolerant, less judgmental, more accepting, more compassionate, and more constructive attitudes toward patients with AIDS, we could help this nation move more swiftly toward the changes that must come if we are to control this scourge. As forcibly pointed out by Theodore Cooper, the president must take the lead.

It was agreed that clear, sympathetic leadership coupled with tough, no-nonsense ground rules that show we are serious about protecting and caring for those with HIV infection and that are supported by adequate financing can get the job done. Examples from history demonstrate that self-destructive behavior can change—not easily, but it can change (as witnessed by the changes in smoking behavior over the past twenty-five years). Further, there is increasing evidence that the gay population and those who are IV drug users are beginning to change their own self-destructive behavior.[1] Clearly, we must continue to pursue the biomedical leads that in the final analysis are our only means of eventually controlling this disease. But we must at the same time put enormous effort into attempting to change both risky behaviors and the attitudes of those who must care for HIV-infected people if we are to come through this emergency true to our heritage as a humane and caring nation.

Notes

1. M.H. Becker and J.G. Joseph, "AIDS and Behavioral Change to Reduce the Risk: A Review," *American Journal of Public Health* 78 (1988): 394–410.

About the Contributors

Robert J. Blendon, Sc.D., is Professor and Chairman, Department of Health Policy and Management, School of Public Health, Harvard University.

Troyen A. Brennan, M.D., J.D., M.P.H., is Assistant Professor, Harvard Medical School and Lecturer, Harvard Law School.

Theodore Cooper, M.D., Ph.D., is Chairman of the Board and CEO, Upjohn Company.

Karen Donelan, Ed.M., is Research Specialist, Department of Health Policy and Management, School of Public Health, Harvard University.

Gayling Gee, R.N., is Director, Ambulatory Care Nursing, San Francisco General Hospital.

Eli Ginzberg, Ph.D., is Director, Conservation of Human Resources, Columbia University.

Richard N. Gottfried, J.D., is Chairman of the New York State Assembly Committee on Health.

Thomas Killip, M.D., is Executive Vice President, Beth Israel Medical Center.

Kenneth M. Ludmerer, M.D., is Associate Professor of Medicine, Department of Internal Medicine, School of Medicine and Associate Professor of History, Faculty of Arts and Sciences, Washington University.

David E. Rogers, M.D., is The Walsh McDermott University Professor of Medicine, Cornell University Medical College.

M. Roy Schwarz, M.D., is Assistant Executive Vice President, American Medical Association.

Lewis Thomas, M.D., is Scholar-in-Residence, Cornell University Medical College.

Bruce C. Vladeck, Ph.D., is President, United Hospital Fund of New York.

Robin Weiss, M.D., is Director, AIDS Activities, Institute of Medicine, National Academy of Sciences.

Cornell University Medical College
Fifth Conference on Health Policy

The AIDS Patient
and the Health Professional
February 23–24, 1989, New York, New York

Conference Co-Chairmen

David E. Rogers, M.D.
The Walsh McDermott University
   Professor of Medicine
Cornell University Medical College

Eli Ginzberg, Ph.D.
Director
Conservation of Human Resources
Columbia University

Conference Coordinator

Ms. Diane Rothschild
Cornell University Medical College

Speakers

Dr. Robert J. Blendon
Professor and Chairman
Department of Health Policy and
   Management
School of Public Health
Harvard University

Dr. Troyen A. Brennan
Assistant Professor, Harvard Medical
   School
Lecturer, Harvard Law School

Dr. Theodore Cooper
Chairman of the Board and CEO
Upjohn Co.

Ms. Gayling Gee
Director, Ambulatory Care Nursing
San Francisco General Hospital

Mr. Richard N. Gottfried
Chairman of the New York State
   Assembly Committee on Health

Mr. Maurice Greenberg
Chairman of the Board
The Society of New York Hospital

Dr. Thomas Killip
Executive Vice President
Beth Israel Medical Center

Dr. Kenneth M. Ludmerer
Associate Professor of Medicine
Department of Internal Medicine
Washington University School of
    Medicine
Associate Professor of History
Faculty of Arts and Sciences
Washington University

Dr. M. Roy Schwarz
Assistant Executive Vice President
American Medical Association

Dr. Lewis Thomas
Scholar-in-Residence
Cornell University Medical College

Dr. Bruce C. Vladeck
President
United Hospital Fund of New York

Participants

Virginia Apuzzo
Deputy Executive Director
New York State Consumer Protection

Donald Armstrong, M.D.
Chief, Division of Infectious Disease
Memorial Sloan-Kettering Cancer
    Center

Mitchell Charap, M.D.
Assistant Professor of Medicine
New York University School of
    Medicine

Nancy Dubler, L.L.B.
Director, Division of Legal and
    Ethical Issues in Health Care
Department of Social Medicine
Montefiore Medical Center

Richard Dunne
Executive Director
Gay Men's Health Crisis

Paul J. Edelson, M.D.
Associate Professor
Department of Pediatrics
The New York Hospital-Cornell
    Medical Center

Ezekiel J. Emanuel, M.D.
Department of Medicine
Beth Israel Hospital

Debra Fraser-Howze
Executive Director
Black Leadership Commission on
    AIDS

William Griffo, M.D.
Associate Chairman
Department of Medicine
The New York Hospital-Cornell
    Medical Center

Casey Horan
Association for Drug Abuse
    Prevention and Treatment

Jonathan I. Jacobs, M.D.
Assistant Professor of Medicine
The New York Hospital-Cornell
    Medical Center

Stephen C. Joseph, M.D., M.P.H.
Commissioner of Health
The City of New York

Robert Klein, M.D.
Department of Medicine
Montefiore Medical Center
Henry and Lucy Moses Hospital
    Division

Bill MacCormack, M.D.
Professor of Medicine
Director, Infectious Disease Division
State University of New York

Kathryn C. Meyer
Vice President for Legal Affairs and
    General Counsel
Beth Israel Medical Center

Aliyah Morgan, M.D., M.P.H.
Attending Physician
Department of Ambulatory Care
Woodhull Medical and Mental Health
    Center

Samuel W. Perry, III, M.D.
Professor of Clinical Psychiatry
The New York Hospital-Cornell
    Medical Center

Beny Primm, M.D.
Executive Director
Addiction Research and Treatment
    Corporation

Nicholas Rango, M.D.
Director
AIDS Institute

Carol Raphael
Director of Operations Management
The Mt. Sinai Hospital

Aran Ron, M.D.
Fellow in Public Health
The New York Hospital-Cornell
    Medical Center

Alan Rosenfield, M.D.
Dean
Columbia University School of
    Medicine

Yolanda Serrano
Executive Director
Association for Drug Abuse
    Prevention and Treatment

Victoria L. Sharp, M.D.
Medical Director
AIDS Treatment Center
Albany Medical Center

Doug Shenson, M.D.
Instructor
Dept. of Epidemiology and Social
    Medicine
Montefiore Medical Center

Mervin Silverman, M.D., M.P.H.
Director, AIDS Health Services
    Program
University of California

Thomas B. Stoddard
Executive Director
Lambda Legal Defense and
    Education Fund, Inc.

Deborah Wadsworth
Executive Director
The Public Agenda Foundation

Abigail Zuger, M.D.
Department of Medicine
Montefiore Medical Center
Henry and Lucy Moses Hospital
    Division

Index